# LEICESTER
## THROUGH THE AGES

## by Joan Stevenson

Kairos Press
Newtown Linford
Leicestershire
1995

Copyright © Joan Stevenson, 1995

ISBN 1-871344-05-0

First Edition 1995

*Cover Pictures:-*
*Front : The Guildhall, or Old Town Hall, by John*
*        Flower, in ?1826, and photographed in 1995*
*back : Map of Leicester by Thomas Roberts, 1741*

Design and Layout by Robin Stevenson, Kairos Press
Body Text in Century Schoolbook, 10.5 on 11.5 point
Imagesetting by CDS Typeset, Leicester
Printed in Great Britain by Norwood Press, Anstey, Leics.

British Library Cataloguing in Publication Data. A catalogue record for this book is available from the British Library

*By the same author:-*
A Family Guide to Charnwood Forest (1982) 56 pages, 33 photographs, 5 maps. £2.50
Memories of Newtown Linford and Bradgate House (1994) 64 pages, 37 photographs. £3.50
Bradgate Park, Childhood home of Lady Jane Grey (1994, with Anthony Squires) 60 pages,
    30 pictures, 3 maps, 13 feature boxes. £3.50
John Wesley in Leicestershire (1988, with Robin Stevenson) 48 pages. £1.50

*Also from Kairos Press*
Leicestershire and Rutland Woodlands Past and Present, by Anthony Squires and Michael Jeeves.
    (1994) 160 pages, 49 photographs, 29 maps, 15 tables, 5 drawings. £9.95

All of the above titles are available post-paid from Kairos Press at the address below.

**Kairos Press**
**552 Bradgate Road**
**Newtown Linford**
**Leicestershire, LE6 0HB**

# Contents

# Illustrations and Diagrams

*to my father, Fred Watkin, who was born in Muriel Road, Leicester, in 1910*

# PREFACE

I stood in Regent Road, gazing at Number 100 and noting the date (1851) and the initials JF. Unusually for our inhibited city, a passer-by stopped and asked what I was looking at. "That is the house where John Flower lived," I explained. "He was an artist who drew scenes of Leicester in the early nineteenth century."

My companion had come across Flower's pictures. "I am interested in history," he said, adding that he had travelled widely and was aquainted with many ancient sites. "The trouble is, nothing ever happened in Leicester......"

# ACKNOWLEDGEMENTS

Many of the people who have helped me in compiling this book have done so unwittingly. I have dredged through great quantities of pamphlets and manuscripts at the Leicestershire Record Office and elsewhere, including the invaluable Transactions of the Leicestershire Archeological and Historical Society, and am greatly indebted to those whose specialist knowledge I have thus been able to draw upon.

As one of the first batch of Leicester's Blue Badge Guides, who qualified in 1976, I have valued the support of my colleagues, and am grateful to those historians whose lectures and tours pointed us in the right direction. Some of them (lecturers and guides) are recorded as authors in the Bibliography. I also wish to thank the staffs of the Leicestershire Record Office, the Reference Library, Leicester University Library, the various museums mentioned in the text, and Dr Barry Biggs and Mr Eddy Hughes.

Having lived in or near Leicester all my life, I have had many delightful conversations with people, including my parents, whose memories go back further than my own. The first event mentioned here for which I can claim a personal memory is Leicester's mini-blitz in November 1940, but I have checked many 20th century events with my father, Fred Watkin, to whom I am particularly grateful, and to whom this book is dedicated.

This book was about to be published in 1985, but the publisher concerned ceased trading and the manuscript languished in a drawer while other matters took precedence. Ten years later, changes in technology have enabled a very different production. For this I am indebted to my son and publisher, Robin Stevenson of Kairos Press, who is responsible for the design, layout, and maps.

Photographic Credits: Most of the photographs are by Robin Stevenson, with eight supplied by the author. Anthony Squires kindly supplied the aerial photo of Abbey park on p.91. Thanks are due to the Leicestershire Museums, Arts and Records Service for supplying the copy of the map on the back cover, and for permission to photograph the Roman Pavement at Jewry wall; Town Wall at Newarke Houses; and Belgrave Hall. Thanks also to Maynard and Bradley of Silver St. for the engravings on pages 54 and 88.

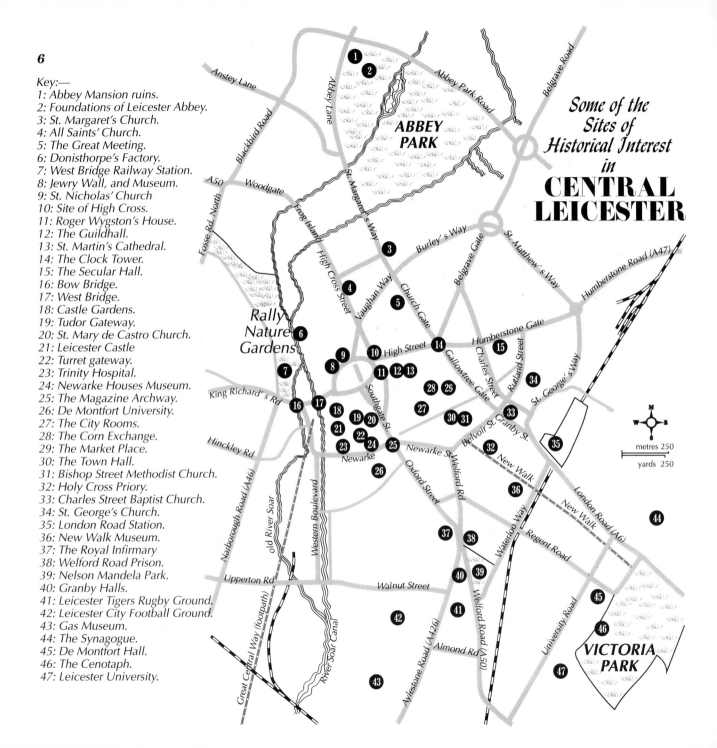

Key:—
1: Abbey Mansion ruins.
2: Foundations of Leicester Abbey.
3: St. Margaret's Church.
4: All Saints' Church.
5: The Great Meeting.
6: Donisthorpe's Factory.
7: West Bridge Railway Station.
8: Jewry Wall, and Museum.
9: St. Nicholas' Church
10: Site of High Cross.
11: Roger Wygston's House.
12: The Guildhall.
13: St. Martin's Cathedral.
14: The Clock Tower.
15: The Secular Hall.
16: Bow Bridge.
17: West Bridge.
18: Castle Gardens.
19: Tudor Gateway.
20: St. Mary de Castro Church.
21: Leicester Castle
22: Turret gateway.
23: Trinity Hospital.
24: Newarke Houses Museum.
25: The Magazine Archway.
26: De Montfort University.
27: The City Rooms.
28: The Corn Exchange.
29: The Market Place.
30: The Town Hall.
31: Bishop Street Methodist Church.
32: Holy Cross Priory.
33: Charles Street Baptist Church.
34: St. George's Church.
35: London Road Station.
36: New Walk Museum.
37: The Royal Infirmary
38: Welford Road Prison.
39: Nelson Mandela Park.
40: Granby Halls.
41: Leicester Tigers Rugby Ground.
42: Leicester City Football Ground.
43: Gas Museum.
44: The Synagogue.
45: De Montfort Hall.
46: The Cenotaph.
47: Leicester University.

Some of the
Sites of
Historical Interest
in
CENTRAL
LEICESTER

# Chapter 1: Ratae

*T*here have been people living in Leicester ever since recorded history began. Before the Romans came there was an Iron Age settlement on the eastern side of the River Soar. Here people of the Corieltauvi (or Coritani) tribe lived in a scattering of round wooden dwellings with thatched roofs.

In the year AD 43 a Roman army of forty or fifty thousand men landed in Kent and the British surrendered in Colchester in the presence of the Emperor Claudius himself. The first task of the conquerors was to spread out and control the country by means of a network of roads linked to garrison forts. The Romans came to Leicester from Colchester, possibly along the line of the Gartree Road, parts of which are still in use as roads and footpaths. The section leading down into the town is now the Evington footpath and the New Walk.

The Corieltauvis appear to have offered no serious opposition, and may even have welcomed the invaders because of trouble they were having with neighbouring tribes. The Romans installed a garrison at Leicester, which they called Ratae, and within a few years, like other garrison centres, it was a thriving town. Local craftsmen set up shops and taverns, and were later joined by retired soldiers. By the time the military withdrew, towards the end of the 1st century, the town was able to continue to flourish, aided by its position on the network of Roman roads. It became the meeting place of the civilian regional council and the place where official records were kept.

During the first half of the 2nd century, a large building programme was under way. A grid of streets was laid out, across which cut the important Fosse Way which, despite its general north-south progress from Lincoln to Exeter, ran East to West through Ratae, probably along the line of the present Silver Street and Guildhall Lane. A basilica was built, combining the functions of town hall and law courts. A new forum, or market place, was constructed. Fragments of the colonnades which surrounded it can be seen in St Nicholas' churchyard and in front of the Jewry Wall.

The Jewry Wall has nothing to do with the Jews, but is derived from the word Jurats, the medieval town councillors who may have met in or near St Nicholas' Church. It is one of the largest fragments of Roman masonry in Britain, apart from defensive walls. It adjoined the public baths, which were built around AD 145. These were excavated after coming to light during preparations for proposed new swimming baths in the early 20th century. To the

*The Jewry Wall, adjoining the Roman Baths.*

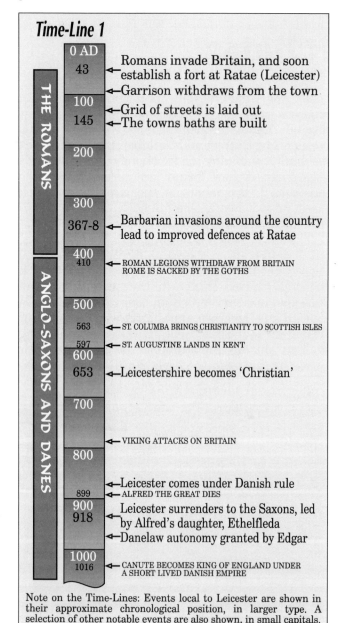

## Time-Line 1

| | | |
|---|---|---|
| **0 AD** | | |
| THE ROMANS | 43 | ← Romans invade Britain, and soon establish a fort at Ratae (Leicester) |
| | | ← Garrison withdraws from the town |
| | 100 | ← Grid of streets is laid out |
| | 145 | ← The towns baths are built |
| | 200 | |
| | 300 | |
| | 367-8 | ← Barbarian invasions around the country lead to improved defences at Ratae |
| | 400 | |
| ANGLO-SAXONS AND DANES | 410 | ← ROMAN LEGIONS WITHDRAW FROM BRITAIN ROME IS SACKED BY THE GOTHS |
| | 500 | |
| | 563 | ← ST. COLUMBA BRINGS CHRISTIANITY TO SCOTTISH ISLES |
| | 597 | ← ST. AUGUSTINE LANDS IN KENT |
| | 600 | |
| | 653 | ← Leicestershire becomes 'Christian' |
| | 700 | |
| | | ← VIKING ATTACKS ON BRITAIN |
| | 800 | |
| | | ← Leicester comes under Danish rule |
| | 899 | ← ALFRED THE GREAT DIES |
| | 900 | |
| | 918 | ← Leicester surrenders to the Saxons, led by Alfred's daughter, Ethelfleda |
| | | ← Danelaw autonomy granted by Edgar |
| | 1000 | |
| | 1016 | ← CANUTE BECOMES KING OF ENGLAND UNDER A SHORT LIVED DANISH EMPIRE |

Note on the Time-Lines: Events local to Leicester are shown in their approximate chronological position, in larger type. A selection of other notable events are also shown, in small capitals.

disappointment of local youngsters, plans for the new baths were shelved.

In a Roman town the baths were a place for gossiping, gambling and doing business, as well as having a wash. It is possible to follow the bather's route from the basement foundations. He (or she) would enter through a door in the Jewry Wall, leave his clothes in a changing room, then pass through a cold room to a steam-heated warm room, where he rubbed oil onto his skin, for the Romans had no soap. Then in a very hot room he would scrape off the sweat and dirt with a metal scraper and perhaps have a dip in a hot plunge bath before returning through the rooms in reverse order, ending (for the hardy) with a cold dip. There were probably segregated times for men and women, though there just may have been some mixed bathing as there were two sets of changing rooms.

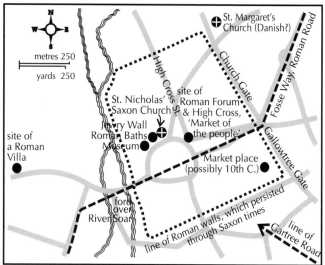

*The main Roman, Anglo-Saxon and Danish sites in Leicester. (The roads shown are those of the present day.)*

The baths were probably in use for about 250 years, till the end of the Roman occupation. How else the citizens spent their leisure hours is uncertain. There may have been an amphitheatre for public sports (generally of a very brutal kind), and a building excavated in St Nicholas' Circle in 1969 may have been a temple. This could have contained shrines to many gods, a mixture of local and Roman. By the year 314 Lincoln seems to have had a Christian bishop, but there is no record of Roman Christians in Ratae.

The large number of Roman-style villas which have been found in the area show the importance and prosperity of Ratae. Nothing of such opulence had been seen in Britain until this time. Some of the rooms had mosaic floors, known as tessellated pavements, and richly painted walls and ceilings. There are several examples in the Jewry Wall Museum. The owners of these elegant houses were most likely descendants of the old Iron Age rulers, now intermarried with the sons and daughters of Roman soldiers, and living like Roman gentry.

During the 2nd and 3rd centuries there was little military activity in the midlands, but in AD 367 there began two years of chaos and disorder throughout Roman Britain. There were invasions by tribes from the north, south, east and west. Ratae may have been cushioned from the worst of the troubles by its inland position, but it set about improving its defences; towers were added to the town walls, and soldiers may again have been stationed in the town.

There was a fire in the central area towards the end of the 4th century, which may have been an accident or perhaps an act of war. Afterwards at least part of the basilica was repaired, but some of the buildings were just left as burnt-out shells, and the forum may have been just cleared of rubble and kept in use surrounded by ruins. The great days of the Roman Empire were over, and defence spending

*Roman tessellated pavement and painted wall plaster, from 2nd century Ratae. These examples are in the Jewry Wall Museum. The pavement is from a site at Blackfriars, and the wall plaster from the Norfolk Street villa.*

*Jewry Wall and Roman Baths. The wall is one of the largest non-military Roman structures in England. Alongside are the foundations of the 2nd century Roman baths, and the museum. Nearby St Nicholas' Church is the oldest of Leicester's church buildings, being in part late Saxon. It incorporates some re-used Roman bricks, and may have been the site of the town's Cathedral in Saxon times.*

had priority over municipal repairs.

Prosperous villa-owners from the suburbs moved inside the town walls for protection. Farms became run down and divided into smaller units. The crumbling Empire could no longer guarantee that runaway slaves would be returned to their masters, and it was the slaves whose work on the land and in the villas made the gracious life possible.

In the year 410 the Roman army officially abandoned Britain. No new imperial coins had been entering the country for several years, and people lost confidence in the money they still had. The economic structure of society began to fall apart. After 400 years of all goods having a value in imperial currency, making trade easy all over the known world, workshops and potteries could only sell locally. Skills were gradually lost, till no-one knew how to make tessellated pavements, or bricks, or window glass, or repair the central heating.

A town cannot raise taxes to maintain its functions when money has almost disappeared. Public buildings were left to crumble, records were no longer kept, and grass grew in the streets.

◆◆◆◆◆◆◆◆◆

Germanic settlers, usually known as Angles, Saxons and Jutes, began to arrive in the country while Britain was still under Roman rule. Within a century of the Romans leaving there was widespread colonisation as the newcomers made their way along rivers and, to a lesser extent, roads and tracks. The old British population was not wiped out, or shunted into the Welsh hills by advancing hordes. It is more likely that there was a slow absorption of several waves of immigrants, sometimes involving fighting, and the eventual emergence of an Anglo-Saxon people.

The centuries following the Roman withdrawal are traditionally known as the Dark Ages, and nowhere was the darkness deeper than in the midlands, where scarcely anything happened which came to the notice of the few chroniclers of the time. Slowly archeologists are beginning to piece together the life-style of the people. The 'darkness' of the age refers, of course, to our lack of knowledge of the period. The people themselves were not living any kind of shadowy half-life. They seem to have had a successful, self-maintaining peasant economy, keeping themselves well-fed, warm and comfortable, and usually healthy. They did not concern themselves with the complications of town life: markets, long-distance trade, taxes, money, record-keeping. Instead they carried on a pattern of local self-reliance which had more in common with the late Iron Age than with the centralised, urban structure of the intervening Roman years.

Although Leicester gradually lost the functions of a town, it was not abandoned, and the Roman walls were still standing and capable of being patched up in the Middle Ages. Very few medieval streets followed the Roman pattern, though, and the grid system disappeared. Not until the 19th century did the inhabitants of Leicester regain a standard of civilisation in any way comparable to that of Ratae, 1500 years before.

Although Christianity became the official religion of the Roman Empire, in such a remote outpost as Britain it may have been confined to the upper classes and to certain areas. It does not appear to have persisted in places where the Anglo-Saxons settled. It was re-introduced in the 7th century, both from the Mediterranean and from the Celtic regions of Northern Britain and Ireland, where it had survived. Leicestershire became officially Christian in 653 after Peada, who was ruling the Middle Angles on behalf of his father, King Penda of Mercia, wanted to marry a Northumbrian princess. The lady's father insisted that Peada become a Christian, so four missionaries were invited to come to the area. A monastery was founded at Breedon as an offshoot of Peterborough, to carry out pastoral work and bring about the conversion of the area.

Leicester became the seat of a new bishopric to serve the Middle Angles for a time. Its cathedral church may have been St Nicholas'. Foundations joining it to the Jewry Wall suggest a building earlier than the present late-Saxon church, and one possibly entered through the Jewry Wall arches.

With the coming of Christianity, literacy increased and Britain again had at least a foothold on European culture. It seems that Leicester was once more growing in importance, and the name Ratae was no longer used. It was replaced by a new Latinised name, Legorensis Civitas, which later developed into Ligera Ceaster, and eventually Leicester.

◆◆◆◆◆◆◆◆

In the late 9th century there was a build up of raids on Britain by Scandinavian people often known as Vikings. Mercia was eventually overcome and Leicester became part of the Danelaw. This was a political region, occupied by Danish armies, which covered much of eastern England. It stretched as far as the Watling Street (now the A5), leaving a marked difference in speech between Leicestershire and counties to the south, such as Warwickshire and Northamptonshire. In Leicestershire English and Danish languages mingled. The commonly used word 'mucky', for instance, meaning dirty, is derived from a Scandinavian word for 'dark'.

Beyond the old eastern wall of the town, a number of important roads bear names derived from the Norse word gata, meaning street: Belgrave Gate, Humberstone Gate, Church Gate (leading to St Margaret's Church), Gallowtree Gate, Sanvey Gate (from Sancta Via, or Holy Way, also leading to St Margaret's Church). It has been suggested that these roads represent a Danish colony outside the Saxon town and served by its own church on the site of the present St Margaret's, which has always been the 'odd one out' of the town's ancient churches. Built outside the town walls, it belonged to the diocese of Lincoln, the ecclesiastical capital of the Danelaw, and privileges held by the Bishop of Lincoln's estate, including the town's east field, were a source of grievance to the council right down to the 19th century.

*St. Margaret's, although outside the town walls, is one of Leicester's most ancient church locations, and may have been established to serve the Danish community. The present building was begun in 1168, but was substantially rebuilt in the 15th century, with the addition of the present soaring tower. It remains the most architecturally impressive of Leicester's medieval churches.*

At some time, probably in the 10th century, a new market was established just inside the eastern wall of the town. This would have been convenient for the Danish community, and is approached by a street called Cheapside, which is derived from the Old Danish word kjøpe, pronounced chirper, which means 'to buy'. Whatever its origin, the market has served Leicester well for the last thousand years.

Danish advances on southern England were halted by King Alfred. When his son Edward became king, the English began to reconquer the territories held by the Danes. Leicester surrendered to Alfred's daughter, Ethelfleda, in 918. According to tradition, the army at Leicester swore loyalty to Ethelfleda, allowing her to strengthen the town defences.

The area surrounding the town became the county of Leicestershire. It remained down the centuries a model shire, with its county town in the centre, unrivalled in size or importance by any other settlement, and within a day's walk of virtually every village in the county.

During the century and a half after Alfred, England suffered repeated Viking attacks, and all kinds of internal division and betrayals. This left the country very vulnerable to invaders. Leicester benefited from being far from the coast. Important building work was going on. Parts of the nave of St Nicholas' church are thought to have been built around the year 1000, and St Margaret's, which also has a claim to being the early cathedral, has some Saxon foundations which can be seen under glass at the east end of the nave, on the south side.

# Chapter 2 : The Conquest

*I*n 1066 William, Duke of Normandy, conquered England. The old Saxon aristocrats gradually lost their lands and their privileges, and some areas, such as Yorkshire, were laid waste. In Leicestershire, though, life for most people seems to have gone on much as before.

William immediately set about building castles in the larger towns and along important routes. Leicester's first castle was built around 1068 and overlooked the river crossing. It consisted of an earthen mound called a motte, with a wooden lookout tower on top, and an outer enclosure called a bailey, which contained living accommodation and stables. The castle mound is now about thirty feet high, but it was higher before the Victorians flattened the top to make a bowling green.

William presented the castle — and a large part

*Leicester Castle hall, from Castle Gardens, with the spire of St. Mary de Castro. The mound is beyond the castle building.*

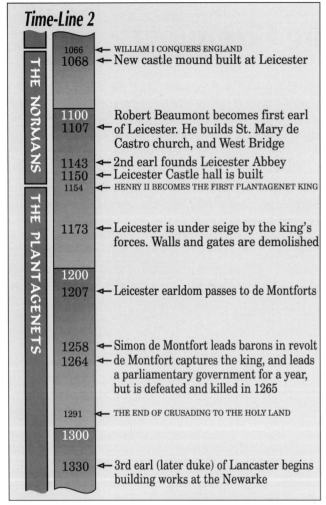

**Time-Line 2**

THE NORMANS

THE PLANTAGENETS

| | |
|---|---|
| 1066 | WILLIAM I CONQUERS ENGLAND |
| 1068 | New castle mound built at Leicester |
| 1100 1107 | Robert Beaumont becomes first earl of Leicester. He builds St. Mary de Castro church, and West Bridge |
| 1143 | 2nd earl founds Leicester Abbey |
| 1150 | Leicester Castle hall is built |
| 1154 | HENRY II BECOMES THE FIRST PLANTAGENET KING |
| 1173 | Leicester is under seige by the king's forces. Walls and gates are demolished |
| 1200 | |
| 1207 | Leicester earldom passes to de Montforts |
| 1258 | Simon de Montfort leads barons in revolt |
| 1264 | de Montfort captures the king, and leads a parliamentary government for a year, but is defeated and killed in 1265 |
| 1291 | THE END OF CRUSADING TO THE HOLY LAND |
| 1300 | |
| 1330 | 3rd earl (later duke) of Lancaster begins building works at the Newarke |

Hugh was included in the council which governed England when the king went back to France. Two years later his wife Adelaide wrote to him from Normandy. Come home, she demanded, or she would look for another husband. Hugh went home, much to the king's displeasure, but managed to persuade Adelaide to come and live in England.

The Domesday Book of 1086 was a general survey of the country made for the purpose of tax assessment. It shows Adelaide as a landowner at Belgrave, Peatling Parva and Barkby, while her husband had massive estates throughout the county and elsewhere. Leicester is recorded as having 320 houses, more than half of them belonging to Hugh, and 65 burgesses. This suggests a population of about 2,000 people.

When William the Conqueror died, his son, the unpopular William Rufus, became king of England. Some of the barons, including Hugh de Grentmesnil, supported the claims of Rufus's older brother Robert (who had inherited Normandy). The rebellion was crushed, and Hugh probably escaped punishment only on account of his age. He was 77 when he died, most likely in Leicester, in 1098. His body was preserved in salt, sewn up in an ox hide, and returned to Normandy to lie in the Abbey of St Evroult.

After the death of Hugh, the fortunes of Leicester rose and fell for several centuries according to the fortunes of its current overlord. The castle was destroyed and rebuilt several times. Hugh was succeeded by his son Ivo, who took part in a rebellion against Henry I, and the castle may have been destroyed as a result of this. Ivo died while on crusade to the Holy Land. His estates were given to Robert Beaumont, to whom he had mortgaged his property. In 1107 Robert became Earl of Leicester.

Robert Beaumont was responsible for the building of the church of St Mary de Castro. He

of Leicestershire — to his friend Hugh de Grentmesnil. Hugh was lucky to survive the battle of Hastings. His bridle rein broke while he was leaping over a bush and his horse bolted into the enemy lines. However, as the English defenders ran up with hatchets raised, it took fright, turned round, and dashed back to safety.

established there a college for a dean and twelve secular clergy (that is, he set up a community of priests rather than monks). The church was later altered and enlarged, but some of the original Norman stonework can still be seen on its north and west sides.

Robert also built the first West Bridge in place of the ford across the River Soar. Taxes were raised from the townspeople to pay for it. Henceforth royalty and other important visitors were met at the bridge and escorted ceremoniously into town.

Robert Beaumont was succeeded by his son Robert le Bossu (the hunchback), who is often considered the best of the Norman Earls of Leicester. In 1143 he founded Leicester Abbey. It was an Augustinian foundation, an order particularly strong in Leicestershire. Augustinians were not quite the same as monks. They were a community of priests who lived by the Rule of St Augustine. This rule, as well as demanding manual labour, poverty and obedience, emphasised the need for charity. Because of their social work, the brothers were less cut off from the world than monks.

The building of a medieval abbey was not a hasty affair, and Robert le Bossu did not live to see it in its full splendour. He is also thought to have built the castle hall. Behind the Queen Anne brick frontage of Leicester Castle there remains this stone hall, dating from around 1150. It was built with two rows of timber posts supporting the roof, because builders could not cope with large unsupported spans. During restoration work in 1985 it was found that, though the posts are Norman, the roof timbers were replaced in the early 16th century.

At the end of his life Robert 'took the cowl' and went to live in the abbey. He died and was buried there in 1168. By that time, Leicester had gained a number of substantial stone buildings. There were

*from Leicester Castle, by James Thomson, 1859*

*The Castle hall in the early 19th century, by which time it was a courthouse.*

six churches, at least one good bridge, the castle hall, and, still incomplete, the glorious abbey.

The third Earl of Leicester, also called Robert, was a very different character from his father. He was quick tempered and impulsive, and, because of his white hands, he was known as Robert Blanchmains. His hot-headedness cost the town dearly when he joined a rebellion against Henry II.

from Nichols, Vol I part II, 1815

*Leicester Castle mound and hall with St. Mary de Castro Church, in a picture dated 1795.*

He went to France, then crossed back to England and took refuge in Leicester. This led the king to lay siege to the town in July 1173. After three weeks the town was burned, but the castle still held out. Robert fled to Normandy. The following year the king's forces again attacked Leicester. The Earl was

away, but the castle resisted and only surrendered when Robert was captured elsewhere. He was refused food and drink until his castles surrendered, so the constables in charge of Leicester, Groby and Mountsorrel gave them up. Robert was later pardoned, so it was the town which suffered most. It was fined £300 and the walls and gates were demolished. Many people moved away. The northern parishes of St Michael and St Clement became so depopulated that they were planted with orchards, and these remained until the 19th century.

Robert Blanchmains married Petronilla, who was probably a great-granddaughter of Hugh de Grentmesnil. Their son William suffered from leprosy, and founded a hospital for other sufferers at St Leonard's, beyond the North Bridge. Petronilla paid for the building of the nave of the abbey church and presented it with a long cord made from her own plaited hair. A lamp in the choir was hung on it, and it became one of the abbey's most cherished possessions. When she died she was buried in front of the high altar. Her husband died in Albania in 1190, on his way home from a pilgrimage to Jerusalem.

The 4th Earl of Leicester, and the fourth Robert Beaumont to bear that title, was Robert FitzParnell. He was on the third crusade with Richard I when he heard of his father's death, but before he reached home he had to overcome all kinds of disasters, including imprisonment in France. Robert FitzParnell's cinquefoil device was adopted by Leicester as its own emblem, and continues as such to this day. His death without heirs in 1204 saw the end of the male Beaumont line.

The 4th Earl's sister Amicia had married into the

*Leicester Castle as it is now. Behind the Queen Anne brick facade is the medieval hall, used as a courthouse for over 200 years*

# MEDIEVAL OVERLORDS OF LEICESTER
### Hugh de Grentmesnil (1021-1098) = Adelaide
### Ivo de Grentmesnil (died on Crusade)

# BEAUMONT EARLS OF LEICESTER
### 1st Earl of Leicester — Robert Prudhomme (Proudman) (1049-1118)
**founded St. Mary de Castro College, 1107**

### 2nd Earl of Leicester — Robert le Bossu (Hunchback) (1104-1168)
**founded Leicester Abbey, 1143. Built Castle hall**

### 3rd Earl of Leicester — Robert Blanchmains (Whitehands) (1135-1190) = Petronilla
**died while on Crusade**

### 4th Earl of Leicester — Robert FitzParnell  (died without issue, 1204)      Amicia

### 5th Earl of Leicester — Simon de Montfort the elder (died in battle, 1218)

### 6th Earl of Leicester — Simon de Montfort the younger (born 1208, died in battle, 1265)

# EARLS AND DUKES OF LANCASTER
## and Royal House of Plantagenet
### Henry III (reigned 1216-1272)

### Edward I (reigned 1272-1307)      Edmund Crouchback, Earl of Leicester,
### 1st Earl of Lancaster, (died 1296)

### Edward II (reigned 1307-1327)      Thomas (executed 1324)      Henry (died 1345)
### 2nd Earl of Lancaster      3rd Earl of Lancaster

### Edward III (reigned 1327-1377)      Henry, 4th Earl & 1st Duke of Lancaster (died 1361)

### Black Prince      John of Gaunt (died 1399) = Blanche
### 2nd Duke of Lancaster

### Richard II (reigned 1377-1399)      Henry IV, (reigned 1399-1413)
### 3rd Duke of Lancaster, titles absorbed into Crown

*This stretch of wall, in the garden behind Newarke Houses Museum, is the only remaining section of the medieval walls which once ringed the town.*

de Montfort family, and in 1207 King John bestowed the title 5th Earl of Leicester on her grandson, Simon de Montfort. He lived in France and was too busy rampaging round his own country to visit England, so Leicester had an absentee lord. Simon was killed at Toulouse in 1218 while his sons were still boys.

In 1229 Simon's young son, also called Simon de Montfort, and destined to bring the name to national fame, came to England. Ten years later he was made 6th Earl of Leicester. He married Henry III's sister Eleanor, but later led a revolt against Henry and headed a council of barons who created the first English Parliament, to which the shires, cities and boroughs sent their representatives.

Simon was killed in battle against the king in 1265. Local people had cause to be grateful that, unlike the 3rd Earl, he did not drag the town into his violent politics. He has not ceased to have honours heaped upon him. His statue adorns the Clock Tower, and a concert hall, square and street have been named after him, as has Leicester's second university.

Simon de Montfort may have been responsible for the foundation of Austin Friars by West Bridge. The major orders of friars arrived in England in the first half of the 13th century. The Franciscans (Greyfriars) obtained land near the town centre. The Dominicans (Blackfriars) had to take a less favourable site, but one still within the town walls. By the time the Austin Friars (Augustinians) arrived in the middle of the century, they had to make do with a damp, low lying site beyond the river. The area is still remembered in the name of St Augustine Street, while the locality of the Franciscan Friary is recalled by Friar Lane and Greyfriars.

After the death of Simon de Montfort, his estates were forfeited to the Crown. Leicester Castle was given to the king's son, Edmund Crouchback, who later became Earl of Lancaster. Although the royal connection was to cause much trouble to the town in later years, it also brought occasions of great excitement and splendour.

Edmund himself was too busy taking part in wars and crusades to visit Leicester much, but after he died in 1296 his son Thomas brought all the greatest lords and ladies in the land to visit his castle. He was the richest man in England after the king and some of his money must have filtered down to the coffers of local tradesmen. All the same, Thomas was not popular. Despite being so rich, he often borrowed money from townspeople and was known to drive a hard bargain. In the end he was executed for treason, leaving the town to pay a hefty fine for guilt by association.

The 3rd Earl of Lancaster was Thomas's brother Henry, who was granted the title in 1324. Having trouble with his eyesight, he retired to Leicester and occupied himself with local affairs. In 1330 he began what he called his New Work. This was a fortified enclosure to the south of the castle, and eventually became known as the Newarke. Within its walls he founded a chapel, a clergyhouse, an almshouse and a hospital.

The original Trinity Hospital had a warden and four chaplains, who lived a common life and were forbidden to make wills — whatever estate they possessed must pass to the hospital. The chaplains were each required to wear 'a comely round tonsure', clothes in sad hues, long cassocks and a black habit bearing a badge showing a white crescent moon with a star on the left hand side. They were not allowed to haunt taverns, get into brawls, walk around town without a companion, seek the society of women, or go to the Market Place without permission.

The inmates of the hospital comprised fifty poor and infirm folk. Of these, twenty were permanent residents. No charge was made for admission and they were given a penny a day, plus a new tunic and hood every Michaelmas. When they died everything they left went to the hospital. The other thirty inmates were suffering from passing ailments. They had beds in the nave of the church, and any possessions they handed over to the warden were restored to them if they recovered, but kept by the hospital if they died.

The actual work of attending to the sick was undertaken by five women. If one of the women misbehaved, she was dismissed, but if she was of good conduct, she would herself be looked after for the rest of her life, taking one of the 'incurable' places if necessary.

When the Earl died in 1345 his funeral was held in the chapel of his new hospital and was attended by Edward III and Queen Philippa.

More new works were carried out by Earl Henry's son, another Henry, who was a great

*Trinity Hospital was founded in the 14th century to house the sick and infirm of the town. The building now belongs to De Montfort University.*

warrior. He grew rich on the spoils of the French wars, and made himself so useful to the king that he was made Duke of Lancaster — only the second English duke to be created, the first being the Black Prince, Duke of Cornwall.

The Good Duke, as people called him, had less time to spend in Leicester than his father, but managed to make himself popular. The King of France gave him a precious thorn — said to be from the crown of thorns worn by Jesus at his trial before Pilate. To display such a wonderful relic he built the Church of the Annunciation of the Blessed Virgin Mary in the Newarke, reputedly one of the most beautiful buildings Leicester ever possessed. Like St Mary de Castro, it was a collegiate church and consequently its endowments were confiscated at the Dissolution of the Monasteries. It fell into decay and now there is nothing left except some carefully preserved arches in the Hawthorne Building of the De Montfort University (see p. 37).

*The Magazine, or Newarke Gateway, was part of the Duke of Lancaster's 'new works'. Built in the 14th century, it was the main entrance to the walled enclosure of the Newarke. For centuries it contained the town armoury, and was a focus of conflict in the civil war. Traffic passed through it into the Newarke until 1898. Now surrounded by busy roads, the only access is from the Newarke/ Oxford Street subway. It is open to the public, housing the museum of the Royal Leicestershire Regiment.*

The duke also enlarged the area of the Newarke and doubled the size of the hospital, increasing its endowment ninefold. Two of his buildings still remain: the Magazine and the chapel of Trinity hospital. The Magazine, also known as the Newarke Gateway, was the main entrance to the walled enclosure of the Newarke, which could also be entered from the Castle Yard and from a southern gateway which was destroyed in the Civil War. The Magazine has always been associated with the military, and was for centuries the town armoury, as its name suggests. By Victorian times the Newarke contained a parade ground, drill hall and married

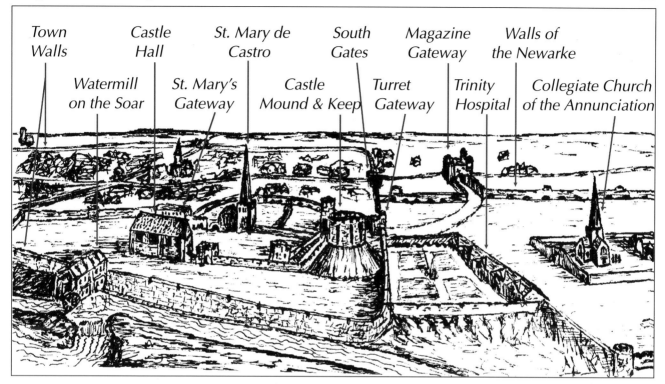

| Town Walls | Castle Hall | St. Mary de Castro | South Gates | Magazine Gateway | Walls of the Newarke |
| Watermill on the Soar | St. Mary's Gateway | Castle Mound & Keep | Turret Gateway | Trinity Hospital | Collegiate Church of the Annunciation |

*Leicester Castle and surrounding area, as it may have looked in its hayday, in the late 1300s.*

*(Based on a drawing by C H Ashdown, undated — Castles in their Glory, No. 7: Leicester Castle in the Time of John of Gaunt.)*

quarters for the militia. It was at the Magazine that Kitchener's army enlisted for the First World War. The building (accessible from the subway network) is now the Museum of the Royal Leicestershire Regiment, and contains its battle trophies and momentoes.

Trinity Hospital, apart from the chapel, has been rebuilt twice, the present building being reconstructed in 1902. Its prized possessions included a nutmeg grater presented by Queen Elizabeth I, and an enormous iron cooking pot, like the ones in which cartoonists boil missionaries. The hospital begged the town for it in 1653 as it was old and disused. The hospital survived the Dissolution because it was seen to be indispensable. In 1995 the residents were re-housed in a new building nearby, and the Hospital building was taken over by De Montfort University.

# Chapter 3 : The Medieval Town

*D*uring the time of the Good Duke, the greatest disaster in the history of Europe struck England: the Black Death. Perhaps a third of the people of Europe died within a few years, and ignorance of its cause meant there was no way of stopping it. Some people blamed an infected cloud drifting across the land. Others saw it as a punishment for their sins and tried to escape by giving away their possessions. What they didn't know was that plague is really a disease of rats. It can only be spread by rat fleas, which carry the disease from rat to rat, or from rat to person.

There had been a European plague in the 6th century, but Britain escaped because it had no rats. By 1348 black rats were all over the country, often living in the thatched roofs of single-story houses. After spreading across India, Asia, North Africa and Europe, the plague reached the south coast of England in the summer of 1348. Increased population and a series of long, cold winters and poor growing seasons had left the people under-nourished, with no resistance to this new disease.

Leicester felt the full force of the plague in the New Year, 1349. In just three parishes, St Margaret's, St Martin's and St Leonard's, 1,480 people died. Work on the Austin Priory came to a halt, and the friars suffered greatly as they continued to care for the needy.

In 1361 the plague returned, and this time it claimed the life of the Good Duke himself, at Leicester Castle, as well as the Dean and seven canons in the college in the Newarke. At the abbey eleven canons out of maybe thirty or forty died.

During this tormented period, the abbot was William Clowne. He was a friend of the king and the duke, a good and upright businessman with a reputation as a peacemaker. He enlarged the abbey grounds and is credited with the building of the stone wall along Abbey Park Road. (The brick wall by St Margaret's Way was built about 1500 by Abbot Penny.)

During Clowne's time the abbey enjoyed national prestige and provided leaders for several other religious houses. After his death there were complaints about the new abbot, though the estates continued to be capably run. The abbey employed a large labour force on its extensive lands, and the sale of its wool was important for the prosperity of the town.

The aristocracy tended to use monasteries and nunneries as retirement homes for their relatives and servants. At one stage Leicester Abbey complained to the king that too many such claims were being made on its hospitality.

The medieval view of life was one of strict hierarchy, with God at the top, and the king, nobles and peasants ranked below. Peasants had to content themselves with looking down on lesser forms of life, such as animals and plants. Some held that a peasant could no more become a lord than a toad could become a lion. Naturally, this idea appealed more to a lord than it did to a peasant, and in 1381 the peasants revolted.

Although the uprisings were in the London area, there was some panic in Leicester. The castle now belonged to John of Gaunt, a younger son of Edward III who had married the Duke of Lancaster's daughter Blanche. When the rebels

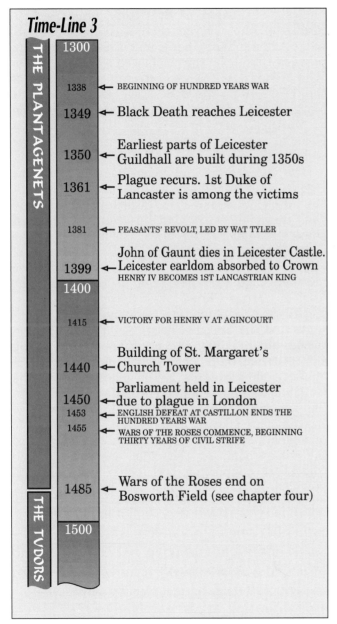

**Time-Line 3**

THE PLANTAGENETS

1300

1338 ← BEGINNING OF HUNDRED YEARS WAR

1349 ← Black Death reaches Leicester

1350 ← Earliest parts of Leicester Guildhall are built during 1350s

1361 ← Plague recurs. 1st Duke of Lancaster is among the victims

1381 ← PEASANTS' REVOLT, LED BY WAT TYLER

1399 ← John of Gaunt dies in Leicester Castle. Leicester earldom absorbed to Crown
HENRY IV BECOMES 1ST LANCASTRIAN KING

1400

1415 ← VICTORY FOR HENRY V AT AGINCOURT

1440 ← Building of St. Margaret's Church Tower

1450 ← Parliament held in Leicester due to plague in London

1453 ← ENGLISH DEFEAT AT CASTILLON ENDS THE HUNDRED YEARS WAR

1455 ← WARS OF THE ROSES COMMENCE, BEGINNING THIRTY YEARS OF CIVIL STRIFE

1485 ← Wars of the Roses end on Bosworth Field (see chapter four)

1500

THE TUDORS

attacked John of Gaunt's London house the rumour spread that they were on their way to Leicester to wreck his castle. An official hastily grabbed the most precious things that came to hand and dashed off with them to the abbey for safe-keeping. The terrified abbot would have nothing to do with them and sent them back. In the end they were stowed away in St Mary's church. The idea of the castle being a secure place seems to have gone completely by this time.

The town was in a state of terror. A story arrived that the rebels were at Market Harborough, so the mayor called on all able-bodied men to meet at the top of London Road hill. Over a thousand men mustered, but it turned out to be a false alarm, so they all went home.

The old Norman feudal system, by which greater lords had lesser lords to service their needs, and so on down the scale, only worked where land was the main source of wealth. As more people began to live in towns and work for money, a new system of local government was needed. Leicester came to be ruled, under the Lord of the Manor, by a mayor and a council of 24 men known as jurats.

The chief traders of the town also banded together to form the Guild (or Gild) Merchant. The function of this body was to regulate trade and industry, and it was managed by the same jurats who managed the affairs of the town. In due course craftsmen such as weavers and fullers formed their own craft guilds. Then there were religious guilds. These provided a burial club and welfare service, supporting members who fell on hard times. They also organised social events, gave charity to the poor, and paid chantry priests to say masses for the souls of departed members.

In Leicester there were at least eight religious guilds, each usually associated with a parish church, and each enlivening the town with an annual

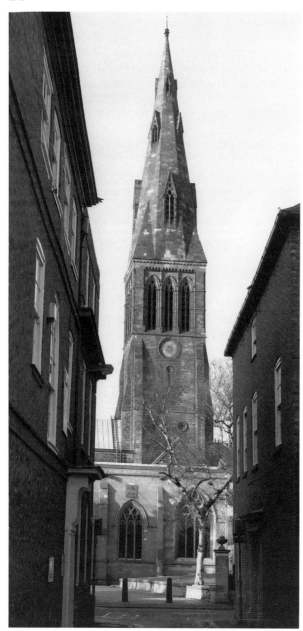

festival. The Guild of St George organised the Riding of the George each spring. St George, mounted on a hobby horse and dressed in armour, paraded round the town followed by a dragon. On Whit Mondays a procession accompanied a statue of the Virgin Mary from St Mary de Castro to St Margaret's. On the way it was joined by groups from St Martin's (carrying an image of St Martin), St Nicholas and All Saints. The festivities always ended with a feast.

The most important religious guild was the Corpus Christi, which was associated with St Martin's church (now the Cathedral). Founded in 1343, its members included the wealthiest and most powerful families in the town. The most illustrious of its founder-members was Sir Ralph Ferrers of Groby Manor. Both men and women could be members, and they held their procession on the feast of Corpus Christi, with flowers and torches and all the civic pomp they could muster.

At first the Corpus Christi Guild met in rented rooms, but by 1390, and possibly as early as the 1350s, it had built its own hall, next door to St Martin's church. This is the oldest part of the Guildhall as it now stands. The hall was extended to the west in the middle of the 15th century, to accommodate a larger membership, so it is possible to compare two methods of timber construction in the same room. At the older eastern end, the framework supporting both walls and ceiling is provided by crucks, which are pairs of curved

*Long associated with the civic life of the town, St. Martin's became the Cathedral when the Leicester diocese was formed in 1927. The medieval structure was extensively restored in the 19th century. The 220 ft. spire designed by Brandon, seen here from New Street, was built in 1867.*

timbers. Using crucks avoided the need for aisle posts to support the roof, but the width of the hall was limited by the length of the crucks. By the following century, when the western end of the hall was built, the carpenters were able to roof large rooms without needing long curved timbers.

Part of the open hearth, from which smoke rose to an opening in the roof, has been preserved. A chimney was built later and is now served by a modern fireplace. The eastern gallery is 18th century and was transferred from the old Market Place Exchange. The west wing, containing what later became the Mayor's Parlour, was added around 1490.

The cream of Leicester society belonged to both the Corpus Christi and to the Guild Merchant. As the Corpus Christi had such a good hall, it was convenient and economical to use it for both Guild Merchant and other town meetings. By the time a properly organised borough council was set up, around 1500, the Guildhall was in regular use as a town hall, and was also the venue for municipal feasts and the entertainment of official visitors. There is no record of any payment of rent for the use of the hall, but there was no doubt mutual benefit, with Corpus Christi members enjoying the hospitality of the corporation.

Although the guild processions suggest a religious life similar to that known today in Catholic countries, Leicester's reputation for religious dissent had its beginnings in these years. The nonconformists in those days were the Lollards, a name derived from a Dutch word similar in meaning to the later 'Ranters'. To their enemies, Lollards

*The oldest part of the Guildhall, or Old Town Hall, is a fourteenth century cruck framed hall. Built for the Corpus Christi Guild, associated with neighbouring St. Martin's Church, the hall was extended in the 15th century, and the Mayor's parlour added in 1563. The upstairs library contains many 17th century books. Its use as the town hall saved the Guildhall from destruction during the Reformation, and it retained this function until 1876. Police cells at one end date from the 19th century. It is now open to the public by day, and also used for concerts and other functions.*

were dangerous heretics, responsible for much social and political unrest, including the Peasants' Revolt. Their sympathisers, on the other hand, saw them as restorers of true, simple Christianity. Many of their ideas were gained from John Wycliffe's new English translations of the Bible from the Latin version, or Vulgate, then in use. There was a great deal of goodwill towards the Lollards in Leicester, at all levels. John of Gaunt approved the anti-clerical parts of their teaching, though he was less impressed by their strictures against self-indulgent laymen.

One Lollard sympathiser who later recanted was Philip Repyngdon, a young canon at Leicester Abbey. He eventually became Abbot, and later Bishop of Lincoln. Unlike some of his kind, he maintained a simple and holy lifestyle, and was never as vindictive towards the heretics as some churchmen. John Belgrave of St Martin's parish appeared before him in 1413 charged with preaching in taverns and other places. Belgrave held original views on fasting. As one meal on a fast day was permissible, he saw no reason why it should not be divided into three parts and eaten as breakfast, dinner and tea. Considering his criticism of Bishop Repyngdon's own career, he was let off very lightly — helped by several important friends from St Martin's who came along to tell lies on his behalf. The following year he went too far and denied the power of the Pope himself. He was sent to prison, together with seven other parishioners of St Martin's.

Another well-known local Lollard was the hermit William Swinderby. John of Gaunt provided his food and he toured the county criticising rich merchants, loose-living women and lax priests. William Smith and Richard Waytestathe also courted trouble. They had to do penance for making a fire with a wooden statue of St Catherine and then cooking cabbages on

it. Three times William had to walk in procession with other Lollards, barefoot and bareheaded, carrying an image of St Catherine, which he had to kiss three times along the route. And worse, he had to hand over for destruction the epistles and gospels which he — a self-educated blacksmith — had spent eight years copying out.

The Lollards believed that religion should be more centred on the Bible and less concerned with outward forms. In an age when Bibles were large, expensive manuscripts which had to be read and explained to a largely illiterate people, there was a particular need for good and wise priests. The Lollards thought these were few and far between.

Ordinary folk found it hard to separate the essence of Christianity from the folk-lore, local customs, witchcraft and superstition with which it was often diluted. When some silver plate went missing in the abbey in the 1430s, Abbot Sadyngton poured some oil on a boy's thumbnail, uttered some incantations, and asked the boy whose reflection he saw in the nail. The boy named one of the canons, who duly 'confessed' to the crime.

A new and impressive landmark appeared in the 1440s, when the 120 feet high tower of St Margaret's was built from the proceeds of a farthing tax on every hearth in the diocese. It remains one of the best Perpendicular church towers in the county.

Meanwhile, the great days of Leicester Castle were coming to an end. John of Gaunt had died there in 1399, and within a year his son Henry had deposed Richard II. Henry, Duke of Lancaster, became Henry IV of England, and Leicester Castle was just one of the king's many houses. Visits were rare.

Parliament met three times in Leicester, including the 1426 Parliament of Bats, so called because members brought wooden weapons in case fighting broke out. On the same occasion the five-year-old Henry VI was knighted in the church of St Mary de Castro. In 1450 Parliament adjourned to Leicester when plague broke out in London. This was a time of upheaval, with Jack Cade and his rebels threatening the King, while across the channel England was losing the Hundred Years' War.

Worse was to come. In 1453 Henry VI became mentally ill and unfit to rule. There was no shortage of people who thought they could do better, and the nobles who had built up private armies during the French Wars now had nobody to fight but each other.

The Wars of the Roses broke out in 1455 between the Houses of York and Lancaster. The Yorkists chose a white rose for their badge and wore it throughout the struggle. The red rose of Lancaster was not seen till the last battle, on Bosworth Field, thirty years later, and it may have been derived from the cinquefoil (five-leaved) badge which the Duke of Lancaster bore in right of being Earl of Leicester. It remains the emblem of Leicester.

With Henry VI deposed, Edward IV became king in 1461. He married Elizabeth Woodville, widow of Sir John Grey of Groby Manor. Elizabeth was the mother of the ill-fated Princes in the Tower, and of Elizabeth of York, whose marriage to Henry VII in 1487 at last united the Houses of York and Lancaster.

Leicestershire was not the scene of any great military activity till the very end of the War of the Roses, and the town continued to be a busy market centre.

At the point where Highcross Street meets High Street some granite sets are laid into the road in the shape of a cross. This marks the site of the High

*High Cross pillar, now on Cheapside. This was originally at the other end of High Street, the centre of the old town, and the same market site the Romans had used. Built in 1557, the Market House had eight such pillars, supporting a domed roof. It was taken down in 1769. The markets combined in 1883.*

*The Saturday Market (or Earl's Market) may have been established by the Danish community in Leicester. For over a 1,000 years it has been a place where local growers and traders have been able to sell their produce and wares.*

The High Cross market dated back to at least the 12th century and probably earlier, for its legality rested in its having been there from time immemorial. It was sometimes called the Townsmen's Market, or the Market of the Community, while the Saturday Market in the present Market Place was the Earl's Market.

The Earl's Market occupied the south-east corner of the walled town. Gaps in the ruined walls, used as short cuts to Gallowtree Gate and Horsefair Street, became recognized rights of way, and remain as what Leicester people call 'jitties.' This market contained areas for selling horses, grain, beans, and so on, with stocks and a pillary for wrong-doers and a pinfold for stray animals. In the 16th and 17th centuries it contained an elm tree, known as the Pigeon Tree, where countrywomen sold pigeons.

Around 1440 a market house was built. Some traders took up stalls inside, but the best trade was always in the open market. Eventually the market house was described as ruinated. Open air stalls were supposed to be cleared away each evening. All market managements feared that stalls left overnight would eventually develop into permanent buildings. This happened in many places, including Leicester, and accounts for the irregular shape of the Market Place today. Pearce's the jewellers forms part of a 16th century encroachment. Over the years the open market place hosted all kinds of outdoor activities, such as election meetings, proclamations, bonfires and public riots.

Leicester had several fairs each year, but they were of only local importance. The two main fairs, held in May and at Michaelmas, were held in Humberstone Gate, outside the restricting town gates. As well as livestock sales, there were always stalls and amusements, so Fair Days were the medieval equivalent of Bank Holidays.

Cross, the centre of medieval Leicester. A market was held here every Wednesday (and in later years, on Fridays as well). There were no market stalls. Farmers' wives would bring along their baskets of produce and lay them on the ground. Rain was a problem, so in Queen Elizabeth's time £100 was spent on a shelter consisting of eight pillars supporting a cupola (little dome). The corporation made a rule that no-one should hang clothes on it. Traffic problems in the 18th century caused it to be sold off in portions, leaving one pillar with an iron cross on top. This remained until the market moved in 1884, and it is now in Cheapside, by the present Market Place.

# Chapter 4 : The Last of the Plantagenets

*I*n the summer of 1485 the people of Leicester had a grandstand view of the end of a dynasty. Two years earlier Edward IV had died suddenly of pneumonia. He left two sons, of whom the elder, at twelve, became briefly Edward V. The country was already torn apart by a nobility trained for nothing but warfare and humiliated by the loss of the French territories. King Solomon would have been hard put to bring England to its senses, and the prospect of a juvenile king was a disaster. Edward IV's brother, the Duke of Gloucester, was informally elected King Richard III and young Edward and his brother were placed in the Tower of London, where they are presumed to have been murdered.

On August 7 1485 the last remaining Lancastrian claimant to the throne, Henry Tudor, Earl of Richmond, landed at Milford Haven in Wales and marched to Shrewsbury with a force of about 6,000 men. His aim was to reach London and depose Richard.

The King had taken himself to Nottingham Castle so that he could move quickly to any part of the country. When news came that Henry had landed, his supporters converged on Leicester from London and East Anglia. They arrived in battle order at sunset on Saturday 20th August. The King himself rode in on a great white charger, with the royal standard of England carried before him. He was in armour, with a jewelled crown on his head.

Maybe 12,000 troops spent that night in Leicester, billeted wherever they could find a space. Richard stayed, not at the castle, but at the town's best inn, the White Boar, named after his own badge. He took with him his four-poster bed, which was set up for the night and then left behind to await further instructions.

*The Blue Boar Inn, by John Flower (1793-1861). Here Richard III spent the night before setting off for Bosworth Field. It was pulled down by a speculative builder in 1836.*

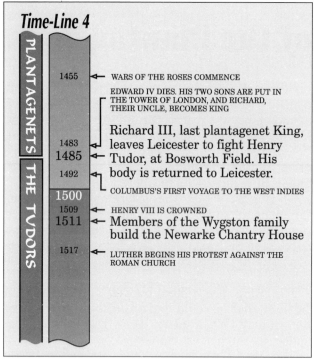

**Time-Line 4**

PLANTAGENETS | THE TUDORS

1455 ← WARS OF THE ROSES COMMENCE

EDWARD IV DIES. HIS TWO SONS ARE PUT IN THE TOWER OF LONDON, AND RICHARD, THEIR UNCLE, BECOMES KING

1483 ← Richard III, last plantagenet King,
1485 ← leaves Leicester to fight Henry
1492 ← Tudor, at Bosworth Field. His body is returned to Leicester.

COLUMBUS'S FIRST VOYAGE TO THE WEST INDIES

1500
1509 ← HENRY VIII IS CROWNED
1511 ← Members of the Wygston family build the Newarke Chantry House

1517 ← LUTHER BEGINS HIS PROTEST AGAINST THE ROMAN CHURCH

The following morning Richard received a blessing from the friars and the cavalcade set off, watched in awe by everyone who was capable of hobbling to the scene. For the last time in England, a king led his army to battle in full medieval chivalric splendour. As Richard rode over the narrow Bow Bridge, his spur struck the stonework, and an old woman in the crowd cried out that when he returned his head would strike the same stone. The aged prophetess was said by some to be none other than Black Anna (or Annis), a legendary witch who lived in Black Anna's Bower, a cave in the Dane Hills which she had clawed out with her own finger nails. This was said to be linked by an underground passage to the cellars of Leicester Castle. However unlikely the tale, generations of children were terrified of having their blood sucked by Black Anna, and their skins hung out on a tree near her Bower.

After crossing the Soar, Richard and his army took the old Roman road through Peckleton and Kirkby Mallory to Sutton Cheney, camping the next night on Ambion Hill. The following day battle raged on what has come to be known as Bosworth Field. Richard III, the last of the Plantagenet kings, was slain, and Henry Tudor became Henry VII of England.

Richard's dead body was stripped and thrown ignominiously over the back of a horse. Then, preceded by the White Boar Herald bearing his standard, it joined the long procession which made its way to Leicester.

At Bow Bridge, Richard's head struck the stonework, just as the old woman had foretold. For two days his naked and blood-stained body was displayed in the Newarke, so that everyone could see that the King was really dead. Then the Franciscan friars were allowed to take it away for a quiet burial. It was placed in a plain stone coffin, and ten years later Henry spent £10.1.0. on a marble tombstone. At the Dissolution of the Monasteries the Friary was closed and Richard's bones were thrown into the River Soar near Bow Bridge. A plaque was erected in 1863 to mark the spot. His stone coffin was placed outside the White Horse Inn in Gallowtree

Gate, where it made a useful horse trough. It was later thought to have been broken up and used for cellar steps. A Leicester Mercury photograph in 1983, however, shows the supposed coffin being used as a plant container in an unidentified garden; another photograph shows 'Richard III's skull', said to have been dredged up from the river when the present Bow Bridge was built.

The victor of Bosworth, Henry VII, came to Leicester after the battle with Richard's crown on his head. He stayed for two days to allow his soldiers to rest and to prepare for his progress to London. The Tudors and their supporters lost no time in blackening the name and memory of Richard III, to the extent that it took the best part of 500 years to rehabilitate him. In place of the villainous hunchback presented by the Tudors and Shakespeare, Leicester displays in Castle Gardens a statue of a lithe and heroic young warrior, presented by the Richard III society.

After the Battle of Bosworth Field, landlords all over the country took down inn signs showing the White Boar and replaced them with something less politically sensitive. In Leicester, where time was short, a touch of the paint brush transformed the White Boar Inn to the Blue Boar. Thus it was known until it was pulled down in the 19th century.

The White or Blue Boar's landlord had also gained a bed, for no-one came to claim it, and 'King Dick's Bed' became a tourist attraction. In the reign of James I, Thomas Clark, the landlord, discovered it had a false bottom. Inside he found £300 in gold coins. He tried to keep this secret, but rumours (originating with his servants) soon began to spread about the man who had once been quite poor, but suddenly had money for anything he wanted. His new-found wealth gave him status in the community and he eventually became Mayor.

After he died his widow, Agnes, continued to keep

*Bow Bridge, over the old River Soar. Meandering channels, and diversions for watermills, required two bridges over the Soar, west of the town, long before the present canal was built. The old Bow Bridge was a precarious looking bow-shaped structure, and it is near here that Richard III's remains were thrown.*

the inn, though everyone knew she was rich. In 1613 she was robbed and murdered. The money was never recovered, but seven men were hanged for the crime and Agnes's maid Alice Grumbolde was burnt at the stake. This was not the end of the story, however, for the ghost of Agnes Clark (known as the White Lady) was said to haunt the Blue Boar until it was pulled down. When a new Blue Boar was built in Southgate Street in 1836, the ghost apparently moved too.

The bedstead has its own history. It was said to have been bought by a servant of the inn who moved

Herricks of Beaumanor, where it became the subject of argument about its authenticity.

The Herrick bed is now at Donington-le-Heath Manor House near Coalville, which is a museum. The ornate headboard and carved posts are considered to be late 16th or early 17th century, but the base might be Richard's. There is no sign of a false bottom, however, or indeed any bottom at all, for the frame is merely laced together with rope. The hangings are a modern reconstruction.

◆◆◆◆◆◆◆◆◆

Leicester was still an important centre for the wool trade. At the end of the 15th century the Wygstons were the town's richest family by far. (Wyggeston seems to have been a 19th century spelling). They bought wool locally and sold it (still as raw wool — the cloth trade came later) around the country and on the continent.

Roger Wygston (1430-1507) was three times Mayor of Leicester and also Member of Parliament. His house in Highcross Street, now the Costume Museum, is probably the oldest surviving dwelling house in Leicester. It is of box frame construction, with two storeys and an overhanging jetty on the upper floor. It was built with the gable end facing the street, but is now buttressed by an 18th century wing fronting the road and a 19th century one to the rear.

Business transactions probably took place in the ground floor hall, where the great wealth of the owner was displayed by a full wall of glass, painted with religious scenes and the initials RW. From details in the fashions portrayed, the windows have been dated to around 1490-95. The painted glass is similar to that in the Mayor's Parlour at the

it to a house in Red Cross Street, where it had to have its feet sawn off to get it into a low room. Then it passed into the possession of Alderman Drake. In the late 18th century, a bed purporting to be King Dick's Bed was in the hands of the Babington family of Rothley Temple. They offered it to Leicester Corporation for the Town Museum in 1831 for £100, but it was turned down. Later it belonged to the

Guildhall, which was built in 1490, so it looks as if Roger Wygston admired the Guildhall glass so much that he ordered some for himself. One of Leicester's resident glaziers, John Malin, was made a freeman of the borough in 1497/8. Whoever the craftsman was, Roger Wygston's windows have been described as being without parallel in England for the period. There are 28 panels in all, probably based on Flemish book illustrations. They show the life of Mary, the seven sacraments and works of mercy, so it does not appear that Roger Wygston was a Lollard sympathiser. The painted glass was removed in the early 19th century and could not now be returned to its original position because of the warping of the window frames. The panes are in the safe keeping of the Jewry Wall and the Newarke Houses Museums, where they can be viewed.

The upstairs rooms of the house were probably the family's living quarters. Since the conversion of the house into a museum, part of the infilling of one of the internal upstairs walls has been left exposed, to show the wood laths plastered with any materials that came to hand: hair, feathers, grit or whatever.

Even richer than Roger Wygston was his nephew, William Wygston the younger (c1457-1536) who, relative to his fellow citizens, was the richest man Leicester has ever known. In the tax assessment of 1524 he paid 22% of the levy for the whole town. This was six times as much as the next richest person, who was his cousin. Like Roger, William was both Mayor and MP several times, and was also four times Mayor of Calais, where he was one of four Leicester merchants who had the privilege of selling wool. In 1511 he and his brothers jointly founded the chantry house in the Newarke (now part of the Newarke Houses museum), where chantry priests were to say masses for their well-being while they were alive and for their souls after death. This practice was swept away at the Reformation, but the

building remained. During the Second World War a bomb dropped in the front garden, leaving the house derelict for a number of years. At length, however, it was repaired and added to the adjoining museum. Inside, the stone spiral staircase, stone mullioned windows, and great fireplace suggest a solid permanence not far removed from a late medieval fortress. William Wygston's coat of arms, painted on stone, was originally over the front door, and is now inside the museum.

In 1513 William founded a hospital for 24 poor folk, called bedemen because they were expected to pray with beads for the soul of their benefactor. For many years the hospital stood close by the Guildhall, where Leicester Grammar School now stands. It was a timber building with a stone chapel. Although it was pulled down in 1875, it has a significant place in the history of building

*Roger Wygston's House. This late 15th century timber-framed building is now part of the Costume Museum.*

| Map of medieval sites in Leicester

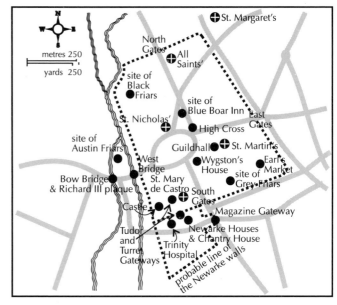

conservation in Leicester. Public opinion was roused — too late to save Wygston's hospital, but poised to prevent threats to other ancient buildings, notably the Guildhall. A new hospital was built on Fosse Road, now in its turn superseded by modern buildings, but still supported by the Wyggeston Foundation.

After William's death, his brother Thomas used part of his estate to establish a Free Grammar School. After various fluctuations in its fortunes this eventually became the Wyggeston Boys' School, with a Wyggeston Girls' School to follow in the nineteenth century. The school traditions are now perpetuated by two Sixth Form Colleges: the Wyggeston and Queen Elizabeth I College on University Road, and the Wyggeston Collegiate on Regent Road.

# Chapter 5 : Reformation

*I*n October 1517 Martin Luther posted a notice on the door of the Castle Church at Wittenburg in Germany. On it he denounced the sale of indulgences to finance the building of St Peter's Church in Rome. Whatever the subtleties of scholars, most people saw indulgences as the chance to buy forgiveness for themselves or for dead loved ones who might be suffering in purgatory. The stone cast by Luther spread ripples far beyond Germany as Europe plunged into Protestant Reformation and Catholic Counter-Reformation.

There had been troubles, plagues and wars in the Middle Ages, but there were certain constant beliefs which provided a framework to life. The 16th century brought both frightening changes and exciting opportunities. The recent voyages to America had altered the shape and size of the known world, while the new printing presses produced thousands of books in the time it had taken to write one out by hand. Luther's ideas travelled fast because he could publish pamphlets for anyone who could read.

Henry VIII had no time for Luther's theology. In his young manhood he had little time for the tedium of kingship, either, and was content to let Thomas Wolsey manage the country on his behalf. Wolsey had risen from humble beginnings by the only route available: he became a priest. He went into royal service and in due course became Archbishop of York and then Cardinal. He was the richest, most powerful, and probably most hated, man in England. For eleven years he virtually ruled the country, but fell from grace in 1529 when he failed to persuade the Pope to annul Henry's marriage to Catherine of Aragon. He was stripped of most of his posts and retired to York. Although he had been Archbishop of York for 16 years, this was his first visit to the city.

Six months later he was suddenly arrested on a charge of treason and ordered to return to London. During the journey south he was so ill that several times he nearly fell from his mule. On Saturday 26th November 1530 he and his escort arrived after dark at the gatehouse of Leicester Abbey. As the abbot, Richard Pexhall, hurried to meet him, Wolsey declared, "Father abbot, I am come hither to leave my bones among you." He was led on his mule to his lodgings, and helped up the stairs to his room.

The abbot administered the last sacraments. In his famous dying speech, Wolsey confessed "If I had served my God as diligently as I have the king, He would not have given me over in my grey hairs." He died at 8 o'clock on Tuesday morning. His body was laid in an open coffin with all his regalia, and throughout the day the people of Leicester filed past. In the evening, the coffin was carried into the abbey church by torchlight, with music and singing and praying. He was buried in the abbey grounds the following day.

In time a strange superstition arose in Leicester. It was believed that killing a spider would cause the ghost of Cardinal Wolsey to emerge from his tomb.

Henry VIII married Anne Boleyn in 1533 and was excommunicated by the Pope. All links with Rome were severed and the king became supreme head of the Church of England. Yet still Henry rejected the doctrines of Luther and the European Protestants. Most ordinary people would scarcely

*Leicester Abbey. Founded in 1143, the Augustinian Abbey of St. Mary's of the Meadows was destroyed at the Dissolution in 1538. These foundations give an indication of the scale of the old Abbey Church, which would have rivalled any of Britain's great cathedrals.*

have noticed that the Reformation had come to England, though there were mutterings by some that now all power rested with the king, he could do anything he wished.

Other countries which had broken with Rome had closed their monasteries and nunneries. Henry saw the advantage of this and between 1536 and 1540 all the monasteries were closed. Their possessions passed to the crown, giving Henry an increased annual revenue of well over one hundred thousand pounds. Now he could fight his wars and run his country without having to ask Parliament for money.

Leicester Abbey and all its possessions were surrendered to the king in October 1538. There was a fleeting hope that at least the abbey church might be spared and perhaps made into a cathedral, as happened at Peterborough. If only the king could have contained his greed, Leicester could have retained one of the greatest medieval churches in the land. In the event, the magnificent structure was torn apart. Bells, plate and ornaments were sold. The lead from the roof brought the king a thousand pounds. The great library of over a thousand books and manuscripts was dispersed. Only the catalogue and a few volumes can now be traced.

The building probably remained in ruins for many years, disappearing gradually as the stones were re-used. Some of them became part of Cavendish House, by Abbey Park Road. This was itself destroyed by royalist troops in the Siege of Leicester, and now stands in ruins.

Eventually all traces of the abbey disappeared. The reconstructed ruins to be seen in the Abbey Grounds are based on excavations undertaken around 1930. There is no known tomb of Cardinal Wolsey, but a monumental slab commemorates its traditional location. The best relics of Leicester Abbey are the walls of its grounds: the stone wall of Abbot Clowne and the brick wall of Abbot Penny. The latter, built around 1500, is the earliest surviving brick structure built in Leicester since Roman times.

The loss of the abbey threw at least 500 people out of work and had serious repercussions on the prosperity of the whole area. Leicester also lost its friaries. Blackfriars and Greyfriars were soon built over. The Augustinian Friary beyond West Bridge was pulled down and the site sold to speculators. In the 18th century coal wharves were built there by the Leicester and Northampton Canal Company. In 1830 it became the terminus for the Leicester and

*Abbot Penny's brick wall, around the abbey, with the earlier stone wall of Abbot Clowne beyond it. It is the earliest known use of brick in Leicester since Roman times.*

Swannington Railway. Trains were advertised as starting at the Augustine Friars.

Henry VIII died in 1547, being succeeded by his nine-year-old son Edward VI. There were changes in the church, for Edward and the faction who controlled him were convinced Protestants. An Act of 1548 suppressed both chantries and guilds. William Wygston had been dead only eleven years when the chantry house, in which priests were to

*This archway is all that remains of the Collegiate Church of the Annunciation of St. Mary, in the Newarke. Built as part of the 1st Duke of Lancaster's enlargement of the Newarke, in 1354, it was reputedly one of the most beautiful churches in England. Like St. Mary's Abbey, it was a victim of the Reformation. This fragment is preserved within De Montfort University's Hawthorne Building.*

pray for his soul for ever, was closed down. The Collegiate Church in the Newarke was demolished and Leicester lost another architectural jewel. The St Mary de Castro college was dissolved, but the church spared. Trinity Hospital, which housed 100 sick and poor folk, was allowed to continue its work.

The social and religious changes were now obvious to everyone. The monasteries were gone, friars no longer walked about the town, clergy could get married. Bibles in English were placed in the churches, and a new prayer book issued. Churches became plainer, statues were taken down, wall paintings whitewashed over, stone altars and rood lofts were removed and organs sold. Fonts remained, as babies still had to be baptised, and all the old central Leicester churches except St Martin's retain their medieval fonts. Early in the 20th century a 15th century wooden carving was found in the belfry at St Mary's. It represented the crucified Jesus being tended by his mother, and was

presumably hidden there at the Reformation.

The Corpus Christi met the same fate as other guilds, but the Guildhall continued to be used as the Town Hall. Its ownership passed to the Crown, and there was a scare when it was sold as part of a job lot to a rich speculator. The purchaser immediately sold off her acquisitions in separate parcels in order to finance further such deals. Happily, the Guildhall was bought at a bargain price by Mr Robert Braham, later Recorder of Leicester, who then presented it to the town. Possibly the speculator was herself outmanoeuvred, for the deeds gave the impression that the property was just a cottage with outbuildings.

Once the building belonged to the town, improvements could be made. The western wing was enlarged to three storeys and a bedroom was

*The Free Grammar School, on Free School Lane, was founded by William Wygston, and built in 1573. After it closed in 1830 the endowment passed to the Wyggeston Schools.*

fitted up for the use of the Recorder when he came to the Quarter Sessions. It had a feather bed and pillows, a wool coverlet, and mats and rushes for the floor. Unfortunately the furniture has not survived, but an upstairs room has been equipped with simple furniture of the 16th and 17th centuries.

The church of St Peter was judged beyond repair and pulled down. Now it is only remembered in the name of St Peter's Lane. As usual, the stone was re-used and came in useful for the new Free Grammar School in Highcross Street. This building, somewhat insensitively restored, is now used as offices. The new school (naturally just for boys) demanded long hours and strict discipline, with much study of Latin literature. The new learning had come to Leicester.

Another benefit to the town came through the generosity of Sir Thomas White, a Tudor Lord Mayor of London who made a fortune in the cloth trade. A devout Catholic, Sir Thomas was concerned by the effects on charitable work of the closure of the monasteries. He bought some of the monastic lands then on the market and, instead of speculating in them like most purchasers, put the income into charitable trusts. These benefited many towns, and in particular enabled young men from Leicester and four other midland towns to receive interest-free loans. They could then set themselves up in business, as he had been able to do when his master died and left him a hundred pounds. Over the years hundreds of young men have taken advantage of this bequest. Loans of up to two thousand pounds over ten years are now available to each of the five towns in rotation. Any resident of Leicester under 35 years of age who wishes to establish him or herself in a chosen occupation can apply. In due course, the town showed its appreciation by making Sir Thomas White, like William Wygston, the subject of one of the statues on the Clock Tower.

The death of the young Edward VI placed Leicester in an awkward position because of its close association with Lady Jane Grey of Bradgate, who was queen for nine days before being deposed by her cousin Mary Tudor. One young Leicester Protestant was burned at the stake in the Catholic years but most people opted for discretion rather than valour.

When Elizabeth I came to the throne, she several times announced her intention of visiting Leicester. Each time the place was tidied up but she never arrived.

The chief personage in Elizabethan Leicester was again an earl; not the Earl of Leicester, for that title belonged to the queen's favourite, Robert Dudley of Kenilworth, but his brother-in-law, Henry Hastings, 3rd Earl of Huntingdon. The Hastings family owned a good deal of land locally, including castles at Kirby Muxloe and Ashby de la Zouch. While still in his teens, Henry had married Katharine Dudley, daughter of the then powerful Duke of Northumberland, at a triple wedding in 1553. At the same ceremony, Lady Jane Grey married Katharine's brother, Lord Guildford Dudley, and Jane's 13-year-old sister Katharine was married (briefly) to Lord Herbert. Henry's marriage was the one happy result of that glittering occasion.

The Huntingdons ran a devout Calvinist household, and Henry soon began to take a prominent part in Leicester affairs. In 1569 he bought a house in Swine's Market (now High Street) and enlarged it into a stately residence, known as Lord's Place. It had two stone towers, and one of these remained, hemmed in by later buildings, till 1902. Mary, Queen of Scots, spent a night there as a prisoner while she was being transferred from Tutbury Castle to Coventry.

The Earl involved himself with all aspects of town life. He supported the Free Grammar School, and enabled several boys to go to University. He set up a fund to buy coal and resell it cheaply to the poor, and re-organised Wygston's Hospital. He also tried, without much success, to introduce new industries.

In Leicester, town sermons were encouraged. In many places sermons were rare events, disapproved of because of the dangers of letting preachers air their independent views. At a time when the pulpit was the nearest thing to a mass medium, many people were prepared to walk miles to hear a good sermon, even though they could be fined for being absent from their own Parish Church.

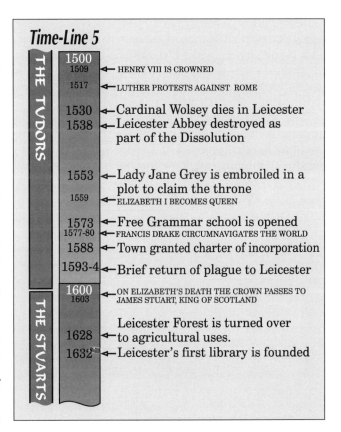

**Time-Line 5**

THE TUDORS

1500
1509 ← HENRY VIII IS CROWNED
1517 ← LUTHER PROTESTS AGAINST ROME
1530 ← Cardinal Wolsey dies in Leicester
1538 ← Leicester Abbey destroyed as part of the Dissolution
1553 ← Lady Jane Grey is embroiled in a plot to claim the throne
1559 ← ELIZABETH I BECOMES QUEEN
1573 ← Free Grammar school is opened
1577-80 ← FRANCIS DRAKE CIRCUMNAVIGATES THE WORLD
1588 ← Town granted charter of incorporation
1593-4 ← Brief return of plague to Leicester

THE STUARTS

1600
1603 ← ON ELIZABETH'S DEATH THE CROWN PASSES TO JAMES STUART, KING OF SCOTLAND
1628 ← Leicester Forest is turned over to agricultural uses.
1632 ← Leicester's first library is founded

Preachers, as opposed to other parsons, were normally Puritans. In Leicester, with its Puritan earl, visiting preachers were welcomed and paid a handsome fee, often five shillings (25p) or more. In later years town preachers were appointed. Far from discouraging attendance, the earl persuaded the Corporation to make a byelaw compelling one person from each household to attend sermons on Wednesdays and Fridays, with fines for backsliders. The Justices struggled to enforce these regulations until well into the 17th century.

Elizabeth made Huntingdon President of the Council in the North, which took him away from Leicester more in later years. He worked as hard for Elizabeth as he had for Leicester, with little reward. As a result, when he died in 1595 he was thousands of pounds in debt. Elizabeth insisted on a magnificent funeral, but would not help pay for it, so his family struggled financially for many years.

The town showed more gratitude than the queen. A portrait was commissioned by the Corporation and painted in 1623, 28 years after his death — a bit late, but showing that his memory was still alive. It hangs in the Guildhall.

At the end of the 16th century, Leicester obtained from Elizabeth its Charter of Incorporation. This provided the town with a corporation consisting of a mayor, 24 aldermen and 48 burgesses. It also gave it the right to make byelaws and to take over some of the old chantry houses, guild buildings and colleges, though these had mainly been destroyed or sold.

There was no money to spare. The long war against Spain and a series of bad harvests sent bread prices rocketing. To make matters worse, the plague returned. A major outbreak in 1593-4 was kept in check by the mayor, who closed the markets to keep visitors away, despite an outcry from traders. About 150 people died, but, unlike the original Black Death, many people who became ill recovered.

The changes in ideas and lifestyles which had taken place in the 16th century can be seen by comparing the two buildings which comprise the Newarke Houses Museum. The western part is William Wygston's Chantry House, built about 1511 for the very medieval purpose of housing priests to say masses for his soul. Next door is Skeffington House, a gracious white mansion constructed nearly a century later as the town house of the Skeffington

*Newarke Houses Museum comprises two buildings. On the left is the stone Chantry House, built in 1511 for William Wygston and his brothers, as a place where priests said masses for their souls. Adjacent to this is the white stucco mansion built as the town house of the Skeffington family in 1600. The museum Includes a 17th century room and a 19th century street, and features Daniel Lambert (Leicester's famous fat man), and Ernest Gimson's furniture.*

family. It looks very different and reflects a very different outlook — less centred on the church, though not necessarily less religious.

A new self-confidence was in the air. Renaissance man had arrived and was less self-effacing than his ancestors. He did not see himself as less than dust, but as a thinking, striving being created in God's image. He was pushing into unknown realms of science, exploring the seas and discovering new lands. Drama no longer meant just mummers and morality plays, but theatrical performances at the Guildhall. People who could afford it wanted to live in greater comfort and privacy, with more space and more furniture.

Many printing presses were set up, and in 1611 the best-selling book in the English language, the Authorized Version of the Bible, was published. It moulded the shape of the language for centuries because so many people learned to read from it. Many of them read little else throughout a lifetime.

The Earl of Huntingdon had established a collection of books in the chancel of St Martin's Church. The books couldn't be borrowed — they were chained to the wall, which was a common practice. New books were bought from time to time. They were mainly theological works, many in Latin, but some in English, and were available to anyone prepared to tackle them. For lighter reading there was Foxe's Book of Martyrs, which was so well used that its chain had to be replaced.

In 1632 the Rev John Angell, Town Preacher and Master of the Free Grammar School, persuaded the corporation to move the books to the Guildhall. Five years later he became Leicester's first librarian. By 1650 he was able to compile a catalogue of 876 volumes, aided by donations from clergy and gentry. Despite his high esteem locally, Mr Angell was forced out of office after the Restoration. He was a Presbyterian, and like many other good men of his time, he was caught in the web of a rigid and inflexible state church.

The library fell into gentle decline, with few additions after the 17th century. Many volumes were stolen or damaged. In 1919 the remaining books were catalogued. Apart from theology, there are works on history, poetry, philosophy, medicine and mathematics. Most of the books are still in the upper room at the Guildhall, but the rarest volumes have been taken to the Leicestershire Record Office. The most famous treasure is a 15th century New Testament in Greek known as the Codex Leicestrensis. This was given by the Rev Thomas Hayne of Thrussington in a bequest of 600 volumes. There is also a New Testament translated into an American Indian language, which was printed in Cambridge, Massachusetts in 1661.

A great deal of work was done to the Guildhall in the 1630s. Apart from housing the library in rooms which were probably originally living accommodation for chantry priests associated with the Corpus Christi Guild, the Mayor's Parlour was remodelled. Wooden panelling was installed, together with the elaborately carved overmantel to the fireplace, which cost the town £23.

# Chapter 6 : Civil War

*J*n the summer of 1634 King Charles I and Queen Henrietta Maria toured the midlands. After being entertained by the Earl of Stamford at Bradgate, they came to Leicester, where the town gates had been painted and householders had spruced up the fronts of their properties. Thirteen dozen torches had been obtained from London to light the streets. The royal visitors were greeted at the North Bridge by the mayor. The next morning, being Sunday, the king attended service at St Martin's, where several rows of seats were removed to make way for a throne.

Despite all this excitement, Charles soon became unpopular in Leicester. For one thing, there was his recurring demand for ship money. This was a tax to raise money for the Navy, which inland people thought was unreasonable. In 1637 and again in 1639 this amounted to £200, which was a quarter of the town's normal expenditure. Then there was the king's decision to enclose Leicester Forest, depriving townsmen of their source of firewood. A charity was set up to provide the poor with coal money at Christmas, but the cost of fuel became a serious problem to many people, and the king was held responsible.

As the dispute between Parliament and the king grew more bitter, and the country grew closer to civil war, Leicester was in a predicament. Such a war recognises no neutrals, and those whose chief desire is to keep out of trouble are likely to find themselves harried by both parties. This happened in Leicester.

The county gentry lined up on opposing sides behind the great families of Hastings, (Earls of Huntingdon), who were fanatical Royalists, and the Greys, (Earls of Stamford), who were ardent Parliamentarians. The borough's two Members of Parliament were divided, one for each side, while the corporation tried to make soothing noises in both directions.

In 1642, as matters moved from bad to worse, Lord Stamford and his servants had an argument

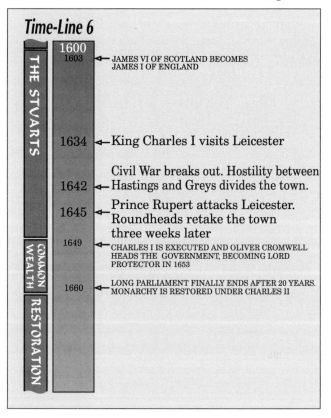

**Time-Line 6**

THE STUARTS

1600
1603 ← JAMES VI OF SCOTLAND BECOMES JAMES I OF ENGLAND

1634 ← King Charles I visits Leicester

1642 ← Civil War breaks out. Hostility between Hastings and Greys divides the town.

1645 ← Prince Rupert attacks Leicester. Roundheads retake the town three weeks later

COMMON WEALTH

1649 ← CHARLES I IS EXECUTED AND OLIVER CROMWELL HEADS THE GOVERNMENT, BECOMING LORD PROTECTOR IN 1653

1660 ← LONG PARLIAMENT FINALLY ENDS AFTER 20 YEARS. MONARCHY IS RESTORED UNDER CHARLES II

RESTORATION

> *The 15th century 'Tudor Gateway' provides access from the town into Castle Yard. The brick infill between the timbers would originally have been wattle and daub. The adjoining Porter's Lodge, built in the 16th century, is Leicester's oldest inhabited dwelling.*

with a royal messenger outside the Angel Inn in Cheapside. Swords were drawn and a fight started. Bystanders, in town for market day, took Lord Stamford's side.

In March, Parliament replaced all Lords Lieutenant with men of its own choice. Locally this meant that the Earl of Stamford replaced the Earl of Huntingdon and the militia was placed under his command.

The king responded by appointing commissioners to raise Trained Bands, who were in effect royalist militia. Lord Huntingdon gave this task to his son, Henry Hastings, who promptly called upon the men of the town to muster at the Rawdykes on June 22nd. A great deal of confusion ensued, but little action. In the end Hastings conscripted about 300 tenants and miners from the family coalfields in Derbyshire, equipped them with pikes and muskets, and marched them down to Leicester. They entered the town with banners waving and a fight with Lord Stamford's men was expected. Swords were drawn, and Colonel Hastings, who had dismounted, was almost taken prisoner. He was rescued by onlookers, remounted and taken to his inn, where the gates closed quickly behind him.

The streets were in uproar, and lives might have been lost but for a providential shower of rain which prevented either side from using their firearms. Lord Hastings left town, leaving his men billeted in local inns. On the instructions of Lord Stamford they were allowed to drink themselves insensible, whereupon they were relieved of their weapons.

The king decided that a royal visit might help his cause. He arrived on July 22nd, accompanied by his son (the future Charles II) and nephew Rupert. They were civilly received at Frog Island, and a respectable crowd lined the streets to Lord Huntingdon's house, Lord's Place, in the present High Street, where they were to spend the night.

On hearing of the king's approach, Lord Stamford and his friends left town suddenly, pursued by some of the king's party, who captured one of them — Dr Bastwick. The Assizes were being held and the king asked the judge to try the doctor immediately for treason. The judge deemed this too provocative, and refused. The townspeople were incensed at the doctor's capture and plotted to release him, but the king had him secretly removed from the area.

Lord Stamford left his son and 25 soldiers in the town, with the task of preventing arms and ammunition in the Magazine from falling into the king's hands. They barricaded themselves inside, with a supply of food. After an exchange of pompous speeches, the king and corporation reached a compromise. The weapons were to be distributed around the county.

On Sunday morning, Charles went once more to St Martin's. Some preparations were made, though many who had previously fawned over him were either aloof or absent. Fresh rushes were strewn on the floor, though, and a gentleman from the Countess of Devonshire's house at the Abbey Mansion set up a throne.

The mayor and corporation planned to attend the king's departure the next morning, but His Majesty did not wait around, and left town before most folk were out of bed.

The king was back in Leicester briefly on August 24th when he stayed overnight with the Countess of Devonshire on his way to Nottingham where, the following day, he raised his standard. This was the signal for open hostilities to begin. The next day Prince Rupert arrived with a troop of cavalry at Bradgate, where he captured some arms and terrified the household. Rupert had recently returned from the continent, where warfare was endemic and not very civilised, and was keen to make a name for himself. One of the uncouth continental practices he introduced was that of holding a town to ransom. From his camp at Queniborough in September he wrote to the Mayor of Leicester demanding £2,000. A postscript added that if funds were not forthcoming "I shall to morrow appear before your towne in such a posture with horse, foot and cannon as shall make you knowe tis more safe to obey than resist his Majesties Commands." It was addressed to his "Friend the Maior of Leicester."

The Corporation were aghast. They didn't know how they could raise so much money. At length they borrowed £500 and sent it off to Rupert. Then they despatched a messenger to Nottingham to complain about the Prince's behaviour. Charles at once distanced himself from such an ungentlemanly kind of warfare and cancelled the demand. The £500 was never repaid, though, and the loan had to be paid off at 6% interest.

As the fortunes of war ebbed and flowed over the country for the next two or three years, Lord Grey ensured that Leicester maintained a garrison for Parliament. Some of the town plate was sold to raise money, but the main worry was the lack of defences. Some banks were built and ditches dug, but it was all rather amateurish. Most of the medieval walls were in disrepair, but the gates were still used. The townspeople strengthened the watch, repaired the gates and hoped that the poverty of the town would discourage either side from bothering with it.

In the spring of 1645 word arrived that the king, who had not been doing too well of late, intended to attack Leicester as part of his attempt to control the East Midlands. On May 29th Charles made his headquarters at Aylestone and his 5,000 strong army encircled the town. During the night his artillery was brought up to the Rawdykes, south of the town. The townspeople demolished some houses outside the North Gate and burned down St Leonard's Church, to prevent its use as a vantage point.

The next morning Prince Rupert offered the town a free pardon if it would surrender. With poor defences and a force of only a couple of thousand soldiers and citizens it might have been politic, if not particularly valiant, to agree. As it was, the Corporation dithered until the farce that had so far characterised the civil war in Leicester slid into tragedy.

A Council of War was held in the Mayor's Parlour at the Guildhall, but no decision was reached. A trumpeter was sent out to plead for more time. Still the council could not agree, and another trumpeter was sent. Rupert now lost patience and didn't see why his men should sit around while the townsfolk improved their defences. He gave the order to open fire. At 3 o'clock in the afternoon the assault began with an attack on the Newarke. Inside the town, the frantic population, including women and children, struggled to plug holes in the wall with bales of wool. Improvised fortifications were set up all over the place, including Gallowtree Gate, Belgrave Gate, St Margaret's Churchyard and West Bridge.

The Cavaliers attacked on all sides and by the early hours of the morning they were inside the town. No-one slept that night and the sounds of pistol shots and clashing of swords combined with the shouts and screams of the wounded to make a din none of the survivors would ever forget.

Some of the hardest fighting took place around the High Cross. Women pelted stones from upstairs windows and hurled tiles off the roofs. The royalists had to fight every step of the way, and the last pocket of defence was in St Martin's Churchyard, where several people lost their lives. Clashes continued inside the church, till at last the defenders saw their cause was hopeless. They laid down their arms and surrendered. Colonel Grey, who was badly injured with two sword-cuts in the face and a pike wound in the back, was taken prisoner. The cavaliers followed up their triumph by rampaging round the town, looting and adding to the toll of suffering and destruction. With the battle ended, the king himself rode into town and set up his lodgings at the Abbey Mansion.

It is impossible to judge accurately the scale of misery brought about by this pointless piece of warfare. A royalist eyewitness reckoned that a couple of hundred people died, and many more would have been injured — many of them maimed for life. 140 waggon-loads of plunder were removed from the town, including much of the corporation silver. Many homes were destroyed or badly damaged, and some people lost everything they had.

Even the king's friends suffered. As soon as Charles left the Abbey Mansion, it was plundered, set on fire and destroyed by his soldiers, to make the picturesque ruin seen today in the Abbey Grounds.

*The Turret Gateway leads from the Castle Yard into the Newarke. Built in 1422/3, it gained its alternative name of Rupert's Gateway, from the civil war events of 1645. The Newarke was heavily bombarded from the south by the Royalist forces, until its walls were breached. The present ruinous condition of the gate however, is the result of 19th century election riots.*

*The ruins of the Abbey Mansion (Cavendish House). Built from the stone of the old abbey, which had been destroyed in the Reformation, the mansion itself was destroyed by Royalists during the civil war.*

John Bunyan, writer of Pilgrim's Progress was a 17-year-old soldier at the time, and by his own account a boisterous and loose-living lad. He was among those detailed to go and besiege Leicester, but another member of the company begged to be allowed to take his place. He agreed, and his replacement was shot in the head and killed. Bunyan visited Leicester thirty years later as a well-known preacher, and is thought to have preached in the same old house in St Nicholas' Street as John Wesley did a century later.

The capture of Leicester was a minor victory for the Royalists, but a major affront to the Roundheads, who decided to counter-attack. The Parliamentary army, under Fairfax and Cromwell, marched on the town. On June 17 they called on Lord Hastings, the Royalist-appointed Governor, to surrender the town. He refused. The next day scaling ladders were brought up, cannons fired, and a breach made in the wall. Hastings knew the place was indefensible, so he and his troops marched out, unmolested.

Within the space of three weeks, the town had been attacked, captured, and then surrendered. Parliament ordered a day of thanksgiving and set up a public appeal for the suffering people of Leicester. The town played no further part in the civil wars.

The execution of Charles I in 1649 led to bitter dissent around the country. Many people who had been no friends of the Royalists felt this was going too far.

The Commonwealth, set up after the death of Charles, tried to remove all mention of royalty in public. 'God save the king' became 'God save the Nation'. Gambling, neglect of church attendance and travelling on Sundays were forbidden. The clergy were expected to behave suitably, and the Rev Mr Mackernes of St Margaret's was reported to the mayor for being drunk in the street.

During this time George Fox, the founder of the Society of Friends (Quakers), who was born in Leicestershire at Fenny Drayton, frequently visited the town. He attended a meeting at St Martin's where Presbyterians, Independents, Baptists and Anglicans disputed their views. When a woman asked a question, the presiding clergyman refused to answer, holding that it was not permitted for a woman to speak in church. George Fox leapt up and became involved in a heated argument about the nature of the church. A church was not, he declared, an old house made up of lime, stones and wood, but a spiritual household of which Christ was the head. The congregation was thrown into confusion and George Fox left, to continue the discussion later in a public house.

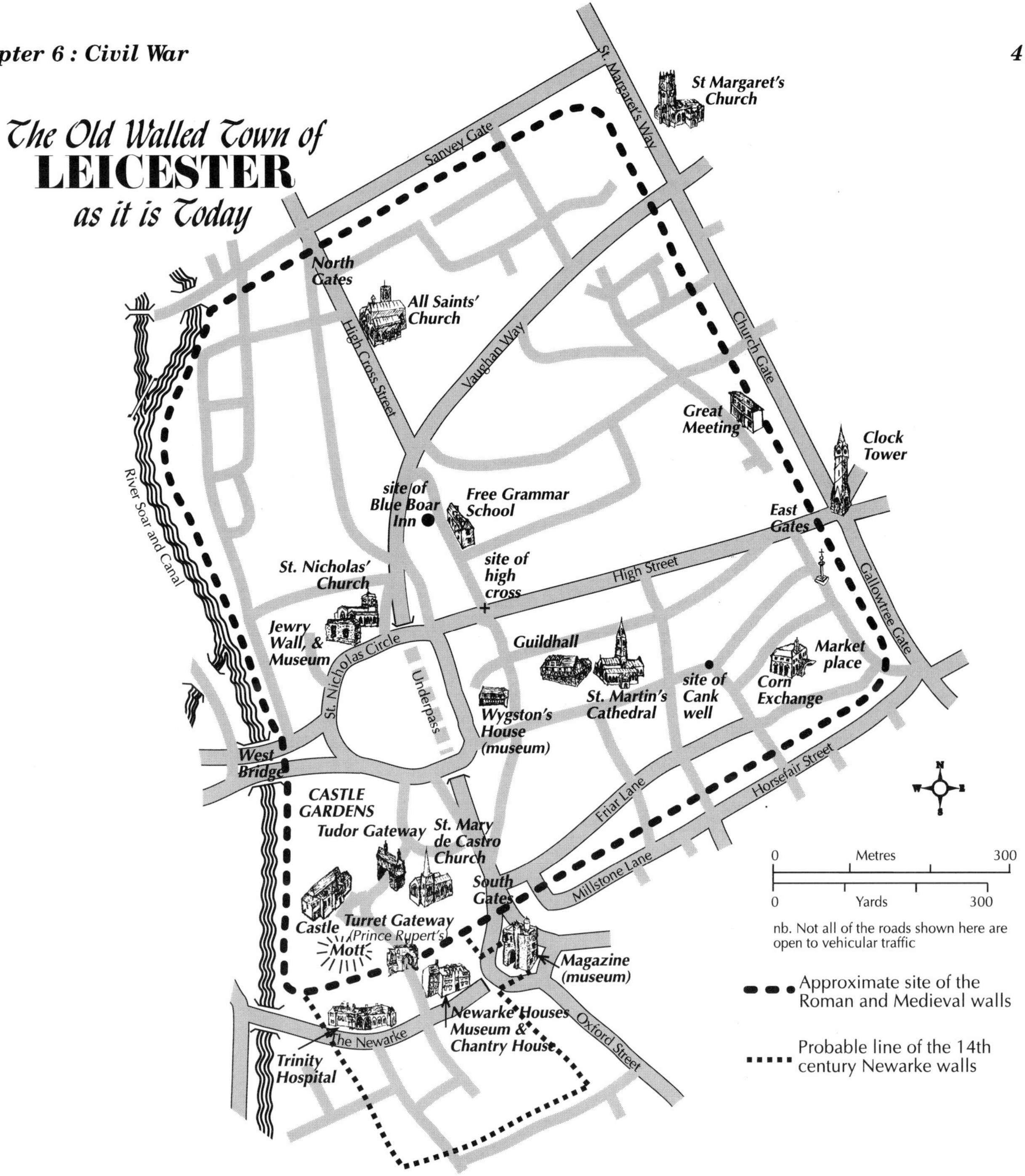

## The Old Walled Town of
# LEICESTER
### as it is Today

St Margaret's Way

St Margaret's Church

Sanvey Gate

North Gates

All Saints' Church

High Cross Street

Vaughan Way

Church Gate

Great Meeting

Clock Tower

site of Blue Boar Inn

Free Grammar School

East Gates

site of high cross

High Street

Gallowtree Gate

River Soar and Canal

St. Nicholas' Church

Jewry Wall & Museum

St. Nicholas Circle

Underpass

Guildhall

St. Martin's Cathedral

site of Cank well

Corn Exchange

Market place

Wygston's House (museum)

West Bridge

CASTLE GARDENS

Tudor Gateway

St. Mary de Castro Church

South Gates

Friar Lane

Horsefair Street

Castle Motte

Turret Gateway (Prince Rupert's)

Magazine (museum)

Millstone Lane

Newarke Houses Museum & Chantry House

Oxford Street

The Newarke

Trinity Hospital

| 0 | Metres | 300 |
| 0 | Yards | 300 |

nb. Not all of the roads shown here are open to vehicular traffic

▪▪▪ Approximate site of the Roman and Medieval walls

···· Probable line of the 14th century Newarke walls

# Chapter 7 : Restoration

*I*n 1660 the monarchy and the Church of England were restored. Charles II was proclaimed at the High Cross, Bear Hill (near the Clock Tower) and in the Market Place. A man called William Dawes was put in the stocks for throwing a clod of earth at the royal arms, and a few people went to prison rather than take an oath of allegiance, but the mayor dismissed them all as fanatics and the corporation spent a lot of money on a feast.

Fifteen years after the siege, many buildings were still not repaired, and the town was very run down. Its only importance was as a market centre and county town, yet even the markets were poor. There was no longer a Friday market at all. The corporation was in debt and there was no important personage to bring in free-spending visitors. Things were looking bad. It could not be foreseen that the coming of the stocking-frame would soon herald a new industrial future.

In the meantime, at least England could be merry again now that activities like drama and dancing were allowed. The Commonwealth had banned all plays, and any actor who tried to arrange a performance was likely to be whipped as a rogue and a vagabond. Under the Restoration, not only did drama re-appear, but much of it was so bawdy that only recently has it been staged again.

The Puritans were also opposed to the May Games, which took place throughout the month of May. Earlier there had been riots in the town when the authorities tore down the maypoles. Morris dancing, too, had been banned. John of Gaunt has been credited with introducing it from Spain in 1332, so it may have come early to Leicester.

Now that pleasure was no longer a sin, houses could become more comfortable. Charles II had enjoyed continental standards of household luxury during his years of exile, and introduced a taste for more varied and elaborate furniture and soft furnishings among those who could afford them.

The panelled room in the Newarke Houses Museum (to the right of the entrance hall) shows how a well-to-do family might have lived around 1670-80. The stone fireplace, discovered some years ago behind one of Victorian marble, would have provided much of the light, as well as the heat, in the dark evenings. Most of the furniture came from Beaumanor Hall. There is a Leicestershire dresser, and a locked side-cupboard for valuable items like

## Time-Line 7

**THE RESTORATION**

- 1660 — MONARCHY IS RESTORED UNDER CHARLES II
- 1665-6 — PLAGUE AND THEN GREAT FIRE IN LONDON
- Stocking Frame knitting industry begins to get established in the town
- 1688 — WILLIAM AND MARY REPLACE JAMES II AFTER THE 'GLORIOUS BLOODLESS REVOLUTION'

**GEORGIANS**

- 1700 — Great Meeting is built, a joint church
- 1708 — of presbyterians and independents
- 1710 — Belgrave Hall is built
- 1714 — WITH NO DIRECT STUART HEIR, THE BRITISH CROWN GOES TO GEORGE I, OF HANOVER. GOVERNMENT BY PARLIAMENTARY PARTY BEGINS

linen, for which the lady of the house would keep the key. The Dutch influence brought back by Charles can be seen in the rush-seated chair and (most unpuritanical) the day-bed. A suit of armour was a fashionable item of decoration, with its suggestion of a warrior ancestor.

The death of Charles brought his Catholic brother James II to the throne. He was not popular in Leicester, or most other places. When it was proposed in February 1688 that the council should send him a loyal address, the motion was defeated by 34 votes to 19 — an unheard-of rebuff. Shortly afterwards the king dismissed 11 aldermen and 16 councillors. These were replaced, but at a further attempt to send a loyal address only three people voted in favour.

In November 1688 William, Prince of Orange, landed in Torbay and civil war again seemed imminent. The king's daughter Anne spent the night at Lord's Place in Leicester as she fled to Nottingham. On December 23rd, James left the country and the 'glorious, bloodless revolution' was over. William and Mary (the king's elder daughter) came to the throne, followed by Anne. By this time Leicester had settled into a pattern which lasted until Local Government Reform in 1834, in which an Anglican Tory corporation was consistently opposed by strongly radical and nonconformist public opinion.

Toleration was not a characteristic of the 17th century. After the Puritan excesses of the Commonwealth period, the Established Church proved just as rigid. In 1662, as part of a national response to the Act of Unity, 41 Leicestershire ministers were driven from or gave up their livings rather than conform to the requirements of the Church of England. Some of their congregations also left, and meeting houses were set up when this became possible.

Quakers had been meeting in Leicester since George Fox's day. At one time Quakers who lived in St Martin's parish refused to pay the compulsory church rates, but agreed instead to pay twice as much poor rate as other people.

The Baptists met wherever they could until they were able to build their first chapel. This was reached from a passage in Friar Lane, and was not visible from the street.

The Presbyterians and Independents joined together (this was unusual) and at first had meetings in a barn near the present Infirmary. Then, in 1708, they took an important step forward and built the Great Meeting in what is now East Bond Street. This pleasant red-brick building

*The Great Meeting, on East Bond Street, was built as a joint venture by the Independents and Presbyterians in 1708, and became Unitarian a century later.*

became the most well-known dissenting church in town, with an influence (like the Quakers) much greater than its membership. The building is box-shaped on the outside, but inside becomes octagonal towards the ceiling. In Victorian times, when the church had become Unitarian, the interior was altered to make it look less like a meeting house and more like a parish church, with a chancel, choir stalls and side pulpit.

Music was always a feature of worship at the Great Meeting, but in its early days the use of musical instruments was not approved of. The more educated members of the congregation used to write their own hymns. The Clerk was the only person with a manuscript, so he had to sing it out two lines at a time, followed by the congregation. He pitched the key by striking the bottom of a brass candlestick. Later, around 1760, a choir was formed and a collection of anthems purchased. To help the singers, a bass viol was allowed, till eventually, in 1800, an organ was built.

The Great Meeting was one of the first buildings in Leicester to be built completely

from brick, though a new brick castle façade had been recently erected. After Bishop Penny's wall at the abbey in 1500 there seems to have been little use of the material in Leicester for 200 years. Some buildings, like the old Blue Boar Inn, had a brick chimney, but the bricks were probably imported from Holland. Early in the 18th century, part of the South Field was found to contain suitable clay and brick-making became a local industry. The first brick kilns were near Welford Place.

Belgrave Hall was built in brick in 1710 for the Cradock family. Although it is now within the city boundaries, it was originally in the village of Belgrave. In the 19th century it belonged to Quaker industrialist John Ellis, whose family lived there until the last of his seven daughters died in 1923. It is now a museum and illustrates a comfortable middle-class home in the 18th and early 19th

*Belgrave Hall, now a museum, was built in 1710 for the Cradock family. This view from the garden shows the simple elegance of the Queen Anne style.*

centuries. The three storeys are furnished in an elegant, but not grand, manner, which is very different from the that of the Restoration panelled room at the Newarke Houses Museum. There is a delightful nursery on the top storey, above dining, drawing, music and work rooms, as well as a kitchen equipped with every convenience from an oatcake toaster to a series of pork-pie moulds.

The stables contain coaches, agricultural implements, and an unusual wheeled sedan chair, dated around 1830, in which a lady of fashion could be transported through the muddy streets.

The gardens are smaller than in their prime, when the kitchen garden probably stretched to Loughborough Road. The vista from the entrance hall is formal, but on either side gardeners have laid out a variety of delights, including greenhouses, rock gardens, and beds of herbs and native flower species.

The public gardens across the road also once belonged to the hall. This area, by the ancient church and nearby river walk, is now a quiet backwater in a busy city, but pictures in the Hall recall the days when Belgrave was a rural community.

In Leicester, as in its nearby villages, the old timber-framed houses were often thatched, but as brick houses became more common, they usually had roofs of local slate. Because Leicestershire slate (often called Swithland slate after the best-known quarries) is too coarse-grained to split precisely, the slater has to make use of varied sizes. So the slates are graded, the small ones being used at the top, and the large ones at the bottom. For the same reason, they cannot be laid edge to edge, but have to overlap the row below, giving the roofs a rough texture. The Leicestershire slate industry came to an end when the railways brought in great quantities of cheap, light-weight, fine-grained Welsh slate, which did not require such heavy and expensive roof timbers.

Slate, in its heyday, had many uses apart from roofs. There is no finer material for gravestones. Many 18th century headstones are as clear now as the day they were made, and can be seen in all the old Leicester churchyards.

Early 18th century gravestones often display uncertainty in dates between two types of calendar. The Old Style calendar began the year on March 25, while the New Style, used in most of Europe, celebrated New Year's Day on January 1. A stonemason, faced with a date between January and March, often opted for both, such as 1727/8. This ended in 1752, when Britain adopted the continental calendar and made January 1st the official New Year's Day. In order to correct our old-fashioned calendar completely, eleven days were taken out of September in that year, to the consternation of people who thought they were losing eleven days of their life.

*Gravestones in St. Nicholas' Churchyard. The slate ones on the left remain as sharp and clear as when they were carved, 150 years ago. The limestone slab on the right, by contrast, is almost illegible.*

# Chapter 8 : The Georgian Town

*W*hen George I came from Hanover to be king of England, Leicester was still largely surrounded by open fields. Ladies of fashion wore high powdered heads, hooped skirts and high heeled shoes. Men wore thigh-length stockings, gartered and turned down above the knee, and the workmen of Leicester now produced large quantities of these stockings.

Only two gentlemen in the town kept carriages, but several others kept a horse strong enough to carry two riders. A lady would usually ride pillion behind the saddle. Milk was carried from door to door on the heads of women, and bread was put in panniers slung over the back of a pack horse.

In 1745 Charles Edward Stuart (Bonnie Prince Charlie) landed in Scotland and marched south with his followers. Charles was the grandson of James II and many Tories, in particular, still supported the Stuarts. Some members of Leicester corporation were openly Jacobite, and aldermen were known to go down on their knees to drink the Pretender's health. They had a fund of Jacobite songs. A slightly later one, which survives, refers to an election candidate of whom they disapproved:

> *As I was going to the Blue Bell*
> *I met Major Mitford going to hell.*
> *I gave him a kick, and bade him get in*
> *To make room for his damn'd Hanoverian king.*

When news arrived that Charles had reached Derby, it seemed that the moment every Jacobite dreamed of was at hand. Not everyone was so happy. Tales were told of fierce, kilted highlanders speaking a strange language, who were quite wild. Some said they were cannibals and went about killing babies.

On December 6 the town was abuzz with rumour. The rebels were at Rothley! They were at Belgrave! Some people hid in terror, or buried their treasures and fled the town. The Jacobites, on the other hand, set about preparing a speech of welcome and organised food for the troops.

At length news arrived that the army had turned north again. Disappointed or relieved, the townsfolk settled back to normality. The rising came to an end the next year at the Battle of Culloden. A national day of thanksgiving was decreed, and the corporation arranged a church service and firework display.

Few weeks passed without some festivity or other. There was always a feast after the mayor's election, and a venison feast on August 1st to remember the long-ago defeat of the Spanish Armada. There was a Singers' feast, and a Florists' feast, and a Tradesmen's feast. These usually started about 4 pm and carried on until the early hours of the next morning, with dancing, card-playing, tea drinking and gossip, as well as serious eating and drinking. There was usually plenty for everyone to look at, even if they were not invited.

All ranks of society enjoyed sports like wrestling, jumping, quoits and weight-lifting. At one time, the town's strongest man was a miller from the Abbey Mill. When a famous strong man called Topham came to Leicester with his show, at which he bent pokers, rolled up pewter dishes with one hand, and so on, the local champion accosted him in an inn and called him a swaggering fellow. Topham took the miller outside and threw him in a horse trough. Then he carried him back to the kitchen, hung him up by his waistband from a hook in the ceiling, and left him there to dry.

Bowls was a favourite sport, and the council provided a public green in the vicinity of the present Bowling Green Street. The upper classes were addicted to cock fighting, and working men to football. There was a race course on Abbey Meadows, but this often flooded, so it was moved in 1742 to St Mary's Field, near the present South Fields College.

There were Assembly Rooms at the Haymarket, which were erected in 1750 and soon became a fashionable social centre. County families trundled up to town in their large, heavy carriages, and put up for the night at one of the more respectable inns, so that they could attend a ball or concert or play.

On Shrove Tuesday it was the day for the Whipping Toms in the Newarke. In the morning there was a small fair, with treats like oranges and gingerbread for sale. There were wrestling matches, games of single-stick, and a barbarous sport called cock-throwing, in which a stick was thrown at a cockerel in the hope of killing and winning it.

The real business of the day began at one o'clock, when a bell was rung to warn non-participants to move to nearby gardens from where they could watch. The men and boys who remained armed themselves with sticks and bound their legs with protective hay bands. Then several men, each with a handkerchief tied over one eye, were let loose with cart-whips. Their object was to whip the legs (officially below the knee) of anyone they could reach, while their victims tried to ward off the strokes with their sticks. Anyone kneeling down was supposed to be safe from attack, but the occasion usually developed into a general fight.

Respectable residents became increasingly outraged by the Shrove Tuesday hooligans, but they could not get the custom ended until the middle of

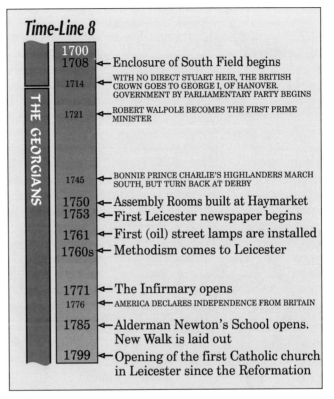

**Time-Line 8**

THE GEORGIANS

| | |
|---|---|
| 1700 | |
| 1708 | ← Enclosure of South Field begins |
| 1714 | ← WITH NO DIRECT STUART HEIR, THE BRITISH CROWN GOES TO GEORGE I, OF HANOVER. GOVERNMENT BY PARLIAMENTARY PARTY BEGINS |
| 1721 | ← ROBERT WALPOLE BECOMES THE FIRST PRIME MINISTER |
| 1745 | ← BONNIE PRINCE CHARLIE'S HIGHLANDERS MARCH SOUTH, BUT TURN BACK AT DERBY |
| 1750 | ← Assembly Rooms built at Haymarket |
| 1753 | ← First Leicester newspaper begins |
| 1761 | ← First (oil) street lamps are installed |
| 1760s | ← Methodism comes to Leicester |
| 1771 | ← The Infirmary opens |
| 1776 | ← AMERICA DECLARES INDEPENDENCE FROM BRITAIN |
| 1785 | ← Alderman Newton's School opens. New Walk is laid out |
| 1799 | ← Opening of the first Catholic church in Leicester since the Reformation |

the 19th century, and then only by Act of Parliament. Even then, the local lads were reluctant to give up their sport and there were several clashes with the police in the Newarke on Shrove Tuesdays. A plaque in the Newarke commemorates this ancient custom, which seems to have been unique to Leicester.

Easter Monday was the day of the Dane Hills Fair. The mayor and corporation, in their scarlet robes and attended by the town waits and hordes of people in their best clothes, walked out to the Dane Hills, west of the town. There was still an old tree there which was said to mark the site of Black Anna's Bower (see page 30).

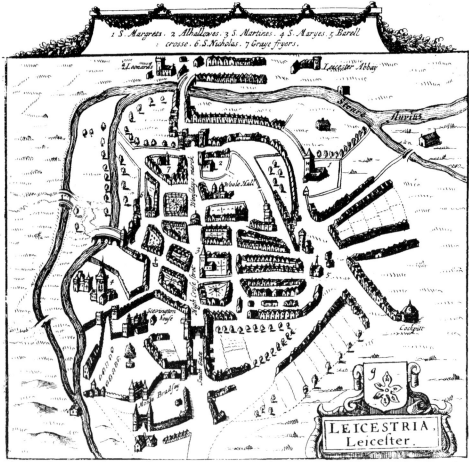

1 S.Margrets. 2 Alhallowes. 3 S. Martines. 4 S. Maryes. 5 Barell crosse. 6 S.Nicholas. 7 Graye fryers.

LEICESTRIA, Leicefter.

*A map of Leicester by Pierre Van der Aa, (1659 - 1733). It shows the town, probably at around the start of the 18th century, just before its industrial expansion began. There are some houses outside the north, east and south gates, but not many. It occupied largely the same area as it had for the previous 1,650 years. It was also mainly a centre for trade and administration. Over the next century it would be transformed into a crowded and expanding manufacturing centre.*

In the morning stalls were set out and games played. Then, at noon, a dead cat sprinkled with aniseed was trailed around the fields by a man on a horse, ending up in town at the mayor's house. Once the trail was laid, a pack of borrowed hounds set off, with horseriders and foot-followers in its wake. The more eminent of the followers ended the day by being entertained to a meal by the mayor. Although the hunt ceased to take place after the end of the 18th century, young people flocked to the Dane Hills on Easter Mondays long afterwards.

Throughout the 18th century there was a long-running dispute over the management of the South Field. This was an area of about 600 acres, and the only one of the three ancient open fields still controlled by the corporation. Common rights in the West Field had been lost with the enclosure of Leicester Forest in 1627-8, while the East Field, enclosed in 1764, was the concern of St Margaret's.

Leicester was still very much a country town.

Though the population is estimated to have risen from about 7,000 at the beginning of the 18th century to 17,000 in 1801, many people still owned livestock and were jealous of their grazing rights. They believed, with good reason, that the members of the corporation were more concerned to look after themselves than to bother with the rights of commoners.

By the middle of the century the South Field was a mixture of pasture and arable land used by several farms. The tenants were mostly councillors and their relations, but it was the ancient right of freemen to turn their animals onto the open pasture between September and February each year.

After several unsuccessful attempts to have the Field enclosed (that is, divided into several parcels and sold), the corporation resolved that after the present leases ran out, the whole area should become pasture. At the same time, new leases were granted to certain aldermen, who undertook to enclose their land at their own expense. Although the rights of freemen were not at this point threatened, they did not trust the corporation. Angry that byelaws should be passed which

favoured the makers of those laws, they marched on the South Field, pulled up the boundary posts, and made bonfires of them. Then they marched back into town and broke the windows of houses owned by councillors. The dispute went to court, and the freemen won their case.

In 1795 there was another attempt to reorganise the South Field. This time there was a surprising lack of fuss about it, despite the fact that councillors were given preference in acquiring some small plots, and the Father of the Corporation had his choice of the larger farms. A significant change had occurred in the town. People were more interested in knitting than in grazing.

The full enclosure of the South Field did not take place until 1811, and an area called Freemen's Common was allotted to the freemen of Leicester in compensation for their ancient grazing rights. This was used as allotments for many years until it eventually became an Industrial estate.

◆◆◆◆◆◆◆◆◆

The growing town needed a better water supply, so pumps were erected over the public wells. The position of the Cank well is marked at the top of Cank Street, near St Martin's Square. The most important water supply was the conduit in the Market Place (near the Victoria Arcade), which received water brought along lead pipes from a spring in what is now Conduit Street off London Road. It was a lead cistern, later covered by a small octagonal building, and the water was said to be especially good for tea making. On special occasions, such as coronations, it was filled with ale or wine.

The first street lights in the town were installed in 1761, when people who lived in Gallowtree Gate

*Site of the Cank water supply. Now marked by a plaque in the road, and seating area, this has been a local meeting place for centuries.*

clubbed together to buy some oil lamps. The idea was taken up by residents of Belgrave Gate and later by some other areas, but most places remained in darkness during winter evenings. People often carried lanterns when they went out at night.

Leicester was moving into the modern world. Its first newspaper, the Leicester Journal, began publication in 1753. Two local radical papers were founded in the 1790s, and this caused the Journal to declare its Tory sympathies.

Education was still poorly provided for, but received a boost from an endowment from a High Tory one-time mayor, Gabriel Newton. Alderman Newton, the landlord of the Horse and Trumpet inn, was a generous but rather eccentric and quarrelsome man. He started a school in St Martin's church in 1747, but it did not last. In 1760 he set up a trust, to be administered by the Corporation, providing for the education and clothing of sons of poor Anglicans. He died two years later, leaving a substantial bequest to the school, which did not open until 1785. It was known as the Green Coat School (ultimately Alderman Newton's). The original uniform was a bright green coat with scarlet facings and brass buttons, leather breeches, and grey worsted stockings.

◆◆◆◆◆◆◆◆◆

It was becoming realised that sick people who lived in bad housing conditions stood a better chance of recovering if they could be moved out of their homes. The main promoter of a hospital for Leicester was Dr William Watts, a modest and remarkable man who trained in medicine at Northampton Infirmary, one of the earliest hospitals outside London. Then he was ordained and became curate of Medbourne. Dr Watts explained his plan for a Leicester Infirmary in the Journal; meetings were held and a subscription list opened.

A site was eventually obtained on the Welford Road, on land which was part of the South Field. The original building, a central three-story block with flanking wings of two storeys, cost £2,200 and was opened in 1771. At first there were forty patients, and those who could walk were expected to help with such tasks as cleaning the wards and washing and ironing the linen. Not all illness qualified for admittance. Hospital was not the place for anyone who was pregnant, insane, infectious or dying.

*Leicester Royal Infirmary, founded in 1771. The original building is shown on the left, with one of the Victorian wings to the right. Modern additions have now dwarfed the older buildings.*

At first there were only two nurses, but it was found that three were needed — one for each ward and one to do night duty with the aid of a night watchman. Advertisements for nurses required that they should be able to read. They lived in the Infirmary, and in the early 19th century they were paid £8 a year. It was a hard life for both nurses and patients, but they were allowed some treats and had a good view of public hangings in Infirmary Square.

Patients had to be recommended by a subscriber, who paid two guineas (£2.10p) a year and could admit two in- and two out-patients annually. Many parishes took out subscriptions so that village people could be treated, as long as there were some tickets left for the year. Soon the whole county was busy raising money for the Infirmary.

In 1774 Mr Cradock of Gumley organised a great musical event in aid of the hospital. As well as hearing a celebrated orchestra, the audience beheld a most unusual sight: Omai, a tall black man in native dress whom Captain Cook had brought back from the Sandwich Isles. He stood up throughout the performance, particularly enthralled by the kettle-drums.

At first the Corporation was conspicuously lacking in support for the hospital, but after 1779 they bestirred themselves to the tune of 10 guineas (£10.50p) a year.

A lunatic asylum was added to the site — treatment mainly being physical restraint, sometimes in chains. A more extensive asylum was built later, and is now part of Leicester University. Genteel sufferers were more likely to patronise Dr Arnold's private asylum in West Bond Street. This was linked by a tunnel to a garden on the other side of the road, where they could take the air without being seen and recognised. Several local notables spent time in Dr Arnold's care.

In 1787 Leicester was visited by the philan-thropist John Howard. He was very critical of the Infirmary, because of its poor ventilation and drainage and its bad management. As a result, some changes were made, particularly at the asylum. Howard was also critical of the town gaol in Highcross Street, and of the fact that the gaoler was allowed to sell ale.

He gave a better report of the County Gaol, where the son of one of the gaolers was Daniel Lambert (1770-1809), who was famous for being fat. Daniel was named after his uncle, who was gamekeeper to the Earl of Stamford and is buried in Newtown Linford churchyard. That Daniel was said to be a heavy-weight, but nobody rivalled the size of his nephew, who was 5 feet 11 inches tall and of normal proportions until he reached his teens. Then, although he did not overeat and was a teetotaller, he started to put on weight until, on the last occasion he was weighed, he reached 52 stones 11 lbs. His servant reckoned he could not have been less than 57 stones when he died.

Danny, as he was known, was a very good swimmer, and taught many children to swim in the River Soar until he became too embarrassed by his bulk. He also had a pleasant singing voice, and at one time worked as a gaoler himself, also helping to support himself by breeding dogs and game fowl. Eventually he had to allow himself to be exhibited in Piccadilly, London, at a shilling a time. He was visited on one occasion by Count Borulawski, a Polish nobleman who was only 28 inches high. They got on well, and Daniel asked the Count how much cloth he needed for a coat. Borulawski replied that he liked a generous cut and allowed almost 3/4 of a yard.

In his last few years, Danny Lambert spent part of his time in Leicester and the rest earning money by making an exhibition of himself. In June 1809 he went to Stamford for the races, and died suddenly in the Waggon and Horses Inn, aged 39. A wall had to be dismantled to remove his body, and it took more than twenty men to lower the coffin into the grave in the churchyard at St Martin's, Stamford. His tombstone, of Swithland slate, records his weight, his waist measurement of 9 feet 4 inches, and his leg circumference of 3 feet 1 inch. Some of his belongings are in the Newarke Houses Museum: his chair, walking stick and clothes; a little statuette of him sitting in a chair; and pictures and cartoons, often representing him as John Bull. He was remembered with affection as a kind, cultured and sensitive man.

A boyhood friend of Danny Lambert's, born in the same year and living next door to him in Blue Boar Lane, was William Gardiner. When he was two, William was sent to a Dame School kept by Mrs Loseby in High Street. This lady, he said, was so old that she could scarcely move out of her chair. She kept a battledore (a bat usually used with a shuttlecock) by her side for punishment. The Gardiners attended the Great Meeting, so later William went to the Great Meeting School, and recalled that the baker used to bring round a basket of hot buns every morning at 7 am.

When William was 19 the French Revolution broke out. He read accounts of this with great interest, going down to the Newsrooms as soon as the papers arrived from London. The Courier, a Tory paper, was available at the Sir Thomas White, which was kept by Mr Throsby, the historian. The Star, which was Liberal, was available at the Billiard News Room in the Market Place.

The French Revolutionary Wars brought one benefit to the cultural life of the town, in the person of an emigré priest who arrived from Bonn in 1793 with his violin and some music. This included a string trio (in E flat, Opus 3) by a 23-year-old German composer whom nobody had heard of. His name was Ludwig van Beethoven. William Gardiner, whose passion in life was music, was enthralled by the piece and made enquiries to London about the composer. He was told that Beethoven was mad and so was his music. It was three years after the string trio was introduced to Leicester that the score was published in London, by which time Leicester audiences were quite familiar with it. Gardiner, who was the same age as Beethoven, became an enthusiastic admirer of all his works, except the final string quartets, which he concluded could only be understood by the Archangel Gabriel.

Gardiner also admired the music of Haydn, and wrote to him, enclosing six pairs of stockings made in his Leicester workshops, in gratitude for the pleasure of his music. The stockings had excerpts of Haydn's music worked into them, but as they were never acknowledged it was feared they were lost during their journey across war-torn Europe.

William Gardiner's mother was a member of the Coltman family, who lived in the house opposite the Jewry Wall in St Nicholas Street, where both John Bunyan and John Wesley preached.

John Wesley recorded in his Journal eight visits to Leicester. On Whit Sunday 1753, on one of his then frequent visits to Markfield, he was persuaded by a gentleman, thought to be hosier John Coltman, to ride the eight miles into Leicester. He preached in Butt Close, near the Great Meeting, which was then an open space. In 1770 he preached in Castle Yard. In an attempt to disrupt the meeting, some-one was sent to shout 'Fresh salmon' a little way off, but nobody showed much interest. His last visit to the town was in 1790, when he was 86 and travelling by carriage rather than on horseback. He came as the guest of John Rawson, one of the trustees of the new Methodist chapel in Millstone Lane — a replacement for the Tabernacle, which may have been the original Grey Friars tithe barn. As the venerable Mr Wesley passed along the street, he replied to those who spoke to him by saying 'Little children, love one another'. The following year he died in London.

Another famous minister, William Carey, came to Leicester in 1789 to take charge of the Baptist chapel in Harvey Lane (so he could have met John Wesley on his last visit). During the week Carey earned a living as a shoemaker in his little house opposite the chapel, surrounded by books lent to him by the town's wealthier citizens. In this cottage he also held a school and did his writing. His slogan was 'Expect great things from God, attempt great things for God'. After four years in Leicester, he founded the Baptist Missionary Society and went to India where, for 40 years, he translated the Bible and preached the gospel. He was also a social reformer and helped to changed the Indian law on 'suttee' — the ceremonial burning of a Hindu woman on the death of her husband. Harvey Lane has now disappeared under St Nicholas' Circle, but Charles Street Baptist Church maintains a small Carey museum, which can be visited by appointment.

Some years after William Carey left the Harvey Lane church, the Rev Robert Hall came to be minister there. He was so popular a figure that visitors were known to arrive on the Saturday mail coach from London especially to hear him preach. His name is commemorated in the Robert Hall Baptist Church in Narborough Road.

The Great Meeting had a new minister in 1803. His name was Charles Berry and he came straight from college, aged 20. His long-serving predecessor at the Great Meeting, Hugh Worthington, had held Unitarian views (denying the divinity of Jesus and the doctrine of the Trinity). Charles Berry was of the same persuasion, and the congregation was split. Some members left to form a new Congregational Church in Bond Street, while the Great Meeting became a Unitarian Church. Its members were less concerned with individual salvation than with the advancement of God's kingdom on earth. They were active in social work and politics, and their influence on 19th century Leicester was enormous. They were less puritanical than the other Free Churches, and even saw no harm in theatre-going.

Churches were well attended, but people did not always attach themselves exclusively to one church or denomination. Eliza Spurrett (later Eliza Stone), who lived at a farm at Knighton in the early 19th century, recorded how she used to attend Sunday morning service at the Great Meeting, then in the

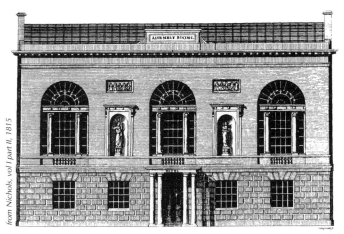

*from Nichols, vol I part II, 1815*

*The classical façade of the City Rooms on Hotel Street. Begun as a hotel in 1792, it opened in 1800 as a fashionable coffee house and newsroom, supplied with the London papers, and later, telegraphed notices of up to the minute information. Upstairs are the elegant Assembly Rooms.*

afternoon she would alternate between Sunday School and Knighton Parish Church. In the evening, she and her friends often walked back into Leicester to hear Robert Hall preach in Harvey Lane chapel, which was so crowded they sometimes had to stand.

Many Leicester people of all church backgrounds supported the Anti-Slave Trade movement, in which the Babingtons of Rothley Temple played a prominent part. There were many meetings and petitions, and some people vowed to give up buying sugar while there was slavery on the plantations. Parliament abolished the Slave Trade in 1807 and slavery itself in 1833.

The Roman Catholics gained their first premises since the Reformation when they built a chapel in Causeway Lane in 1799. Eighteen years later they built a church in Wellington Street, backing on to the New Walk.

Soon the Church of England, too, was building again, for the five remaining medieval churches were quite insufficient for the growing town. To mark the Battle of Waterloo, Parliament established a £$1\frac{1}{2}$ million fund to build new Anglican churches, and Leicester built St George's, near Rutland Street. The Waterloo Churches re-introduced the old Gothic style of architecture, with pointed arches and windows. This soon became the dominant style for 19th century churches, whether of stone or brick. Some influential architects maintained it was the only suitable style for churches as it was based on medieval Christian buildings instead of the pagan 'classical' styles of ancient Greece and Rome. St George's now belongs to the Serbian Orthodox Church.

In 1804 a little book was published, called A Walk through Leicester. Not until nearly forty years later, in the year of her death, was the author revealed to be Susannah Watts, niece of Dr William Watts, founder of the Infirmary. Miss Watts was born in

*St. George's Church, Rutland Street — a 'Waterloo Church' of the early 1800s, it served a rapidly expanding part of the town, and heralded a 19th century Gothic revival. It now houses a Serbian Orthodox congregation.*

1768 at Danett's Hall, beyond the West Bridge, which had been inherited by her uncle, who had sold it to his brother John, her father. John died when Susannah was very young, and she grew up to a life of genteel poverty, with little formal education, but determined to help the family income however she could. In her day she was mainly admired for her landscape pictures made from birds' feathers.

In this early Guidebook (reprinted in a facsimile edition in 1967) the reader is led along a fairly extended route around Leicester, beginning at the Three Crowns Inn in Granby Street (now the site of the National Westminster Bank). Humberstone Gate, we are told, leads to a range of new and handsome dwellings called Spa Place (now offices). Here a chalybeate spring (water containing iron salts) had been found and marble baths installed in the vain hope of making Leicester a famous Spa town. The water was not found to contain much in the way of mineral properties, and the project was abandoned.

In Belgrave Gate Miss Watts points out the Roman mile-stone, brought from Thurmaston. Worried that it might be damaged, she suggests moving it to the Infirmary garden. Today it is in the safety of the Jewry Wall museum. The Jewry wall puzzled her, as it must have puzzled Leicester people for centuries. The land beside it was built over, and no-one knew that the foundations of Roman baths lay beneath. The structure was known to be Roman, and Miss Watts thought, wrongly but not unreasonably, that the name referred to some previous Jewish quarter of the town.

The buildings of antiquity interested Susannah Watts more than the architecture of her own day. Yet around her, new areas of elegant Georgian housing were being developed. In Friar Lane and New Street, substantial brick houses were being built. Gateway House in the Newarke, now overshadowed by the towers of De Montfort University, was part of a select residential area.

The classically styled 'City Rooms', which Susannah admired, was intended to be a hotel (and gave us its street name — Hotel Street), but it was never used as such. She tells us that the ground floor contained a book shop and a coffee room supplied with all the London papers. Upstairs there is still the splendid Assembly Rooms where public balls were held.

The corporation opened up another area of middle-class housing when, in 1785, it laid out a pedestrian walk, originally called Queen's Walk, but for most of its history known as New Walk. There was already a footpath along the route, which was part of the ancient Gartree Road, and formed the boundary between the parishes of St Mary and St Margaret.

The completed New Walk was ten yards wide and

*Spa Place, Humberstone gate, an attempt to cash in on the Georgian fashion for health promoting spring water*

*The Crescent, on King Street.*

just over a mile long, leading from the town to the London Road. Gravel and labour were provided by the corporation, and public subscription produced £250 worth of trees and shrubs. A new racecourse was opened on the present Victoria Park in 1806. The New Walk provided a direct route, and a promenade along which ladies could take exercise without ruining their elegant dresses. Elsewhere in the town, footways were just beginning to be provided, but mostly pedestrians had to share the muddy streets with horses and their vehicles.

Originally there were open views from the New Walk over the South Field, but after enclosure, the corporation made further land in the area available for housing. Homes of good quality were built in King Street (from 1811), Wellington Street (1812), Princess Road (1815) and Regent Road. This district is now a conservation area and contains many classical-style buildings of the Regency and later

*New Walk was laid out in 1785 to provide a pleasant promenade and fashionable Georgian suberb.*

Georgian period, some in brick and others stuccoed in pastel shades. Some of the best are the work of Leicester architect William Flint, whose trademark was a frieze of honeysuckle design. There are some of his houses in Upper King Street, and he also built Charles Street Baptist Church. The Crescent in King Street dates from about 1820 and was narrowly saved from demolition at a time when much of old Leicester was falling to the bulldozers in the 1960s and 70s.

The first ten building plots on the New Walk were on the east side, close to Welford Place. They were sold by auction in 1811 to provide funds to cover the cost of the Enclosure enquiry. Over the years, housing spread along the whole length of the walk, which became a very fashionable place to live. Generally, the further up the hill, the later the building. A wander up New Walk provides an interesting illustration of the development of building styles in the 19th century. The 20th century infill is sometimes interesting, often dreadful.

# Chapter 9 : Framework Knitters and Violent Politics

*U*ntil Elizabethan times, stockings were made of woven material cut on the cross, but when the queen was given some hand-knitted silk stockings she found them so comfortable she would wear no others, and a new fashion was born. A century later the Rev William Lee of Calverton in Nottinghamshire invented the first knitting machine. He is said to have watched his girlfriend knitting stockings on four needles, which she changed to two when the heel was turned. The process seemed very slow, so he set about devising a machine which could make knitted fabric by holding each loop on a hooked needle.

The industry first grew up in London, but the hosiers and the Framework Knitters' Company kept such a tight control, with heavy fees and fines and a restricted number of apprentices, that after the civil war some of the knitters moved to the East Midlands. Stocking-making became Leicester's first (and, for the best part of 200 years, only) industry.

The long-stapled wool from local sheep particularly suited worsted spinning, in which the fibres of the fleece are kept parallel, making a smooth yarn. Worsted Knitting became Leicester's speciality.

At first a knitter generally either bought his own frame, or hired one from a merchant hosier. He collected his yarn at the beginning of the week, and received payment for the completed work on Saturday, with deductions for faults and frame rent. Later, distribution tended to be taken over by middlemen, or bagmen, though some knitters dealt directly with the hosier.

More and more people took up framework knitting, and, away from London controls, stockingers

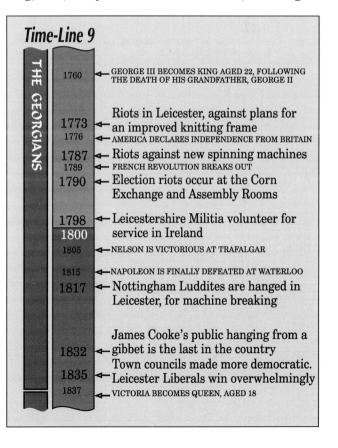

**Time-Line 9**

THE GEORGIANS

1760 ← GEORGE III BECOMES KING AGED 22, FOLLOWING THE DEATH OF HIS GRANDFATHER, GEORGE II

1773 ← Riots in Leicester, against plans for an improved knitting frame
1776 ← AMERICA DECLARES INDEPENDENCE FROM BRITAIN
1787 ← Riots against new spinning machines
1789 ← FRENCH REVOLUTION BREAKS OUT
1790 ← Election riots occur at the Corn Exchange and Assembly Rooms

1798 ← Leicestershire Militia volunteer for service in Ireland
1800
1805 ← NELSON IS VICTORIOUS AT TRAFALGAR

1815 ← NAPOLEON IS FINALLY DEFEATED AT WATERLOO
1817 ← Nottingham Luddites are hanged in Leicester, for machine breaking

James Cooke's public hanging from a
1832 ← gibbet is the last in the country
Town councils made more democratic.
1835 ← Leicester Liberals win overwhelmingly
1837 ← VICTORIA BECOMES QUEEN, AGED 18

were keen to take on apprentices as cheap labour. People with a little capital, such as shopkeepers, publicans and farmers, became small employers. They could buy a few frames and hire them out to a hosier or middleman.

The people least able to afford frames were the knitters, and the few who did have their own frames were unpopular. With no frame rent to pay, they were sometimes tempted to work for reduced rates, depressing the wages for everyone else. As well as renting his frame, whether he had any work or not, the knitter had to employ a bobbin winder and a seamer (or use his family), and to provide his own light, fuel and replacement needles.

As the workers carried most of the risks, the hosiers had little incentive to build factories, so until the second half of the 19th century, knitting mainly took place in homes and workshops. A stockinger at work can be seen in a reconstructed workshop at the Newarke Houses Museum, and there are examples of knitting frames at the Abbey Pumping Station museum of technology in Corporation Road.

'As poor as a stockinger' was an 18th century saying, but times got even worse in the next century. When profits were low, employers looked for improved machinery. This was just what the workers feared, for better machines needed fewer operatives. There were no Trades Unions, and the threat of starvation was real. With nothing to lose, stockingers were easily roused to violence.

In March 1773, two hosiers tried to introduce an improved stocking frame. Rumour spread that it could do the work of sixty men. This was an exaggeration, but a series of bad harvests had brought high food prices and people were desperate. About a thousand men, some from local villages, swarmed into the market place, where the new machine was being exhibited in the Exchange.

Someone threw up a football, which was taken as time for the kick-off, and a riot broke out. The mayor came out and told the men he understood their plight. He tried to convince them of the benefits of the new frame, which they should come and see for themselves. Instead, the ringleaders burst into the Exchange and dragged out the machine, which was soon pulled to pieces by the crowd. The hosiers abandoned their plans, afraid that further trouble would drive trade away from Leicester.

A similar, but more serious, episode occurred in 1787. Spinning was traditionally carried out by countrywomen, but there were townsmen who worked spinning wheels. This is a slow process, so a local inventor, Joseph Brookhouse, applied to worsted the principles which Arkwright had used to mechanise cotton spinning. He took as partners fellow members of the Great Meeting, John Coltman, hosier, and Joseph Whetstone, master woolcomber.

Hearing of this threat to their livelihood, the workmen descended on Mr Whetstone's house in Northgate Street, and then moved on to Mr Coltman's house in Shambles Lane, where they smashed the front windows and gutters. Mr Whetstone, fearing their return, and expecting little help from the Tory magistrates, sent his womenfolk to safety and gathered his sons and friends upstairs, armed with fowling pieces. The mob arrived, many of them drunk, and began to throw stones at the windows. It was an old Elizabethan house with a jettied upper storey, so some of the rioters could shelter under the jetty and get into the ground floor, where they broke up all the furniture. Mr Whetstone escaped down a rope from a back window, crossed the garden and left Leicester on a borrowed horse in the middle of the night. At least one of the rioters was taken to the Infirmary with gunshot wounds.

At length the mayor arrived with a few constables. He is said to have tapped some of the crowd gently on the back saying, 'Come, my lads, give over – you've done enough – quite enough.' When the lads took no notice, he read the Riot Act. He was still reading it when he was hit on the head by a stone, receiving an injury from which he later died. Eventually, the militia were brought in, but the rioting lasted for ten days.

The sad events of 1787 show not only tensions between employers and workmen, but also the rift between the largely Liberal Nonconformist manufacturers and the Tory Anglican corporation, who waited for several hours before responding for appeals for help. As a result of the troubles, worsted spinning was driven out of Leicester for more than twenty years.

The French Revolution, which broke out in 1789, embittered politics further. Whigs at first welcomed the reform of a corrupt and selfish regime, while the Tories dreaded a breakdown of law and order being imported into Britain.

There were election riots in Leicester in 1790. A mob broke into the Exchange and the Assembly Rooms, smashing musical instruments and destroying corporation records. The Market Place was said to be ankle deep in music and official papers. Troops were brought out to restore order, as they were when there were food riots two years later.

As the French Revolution entered its period of Terror, it lost many of its supporters, and many urged war against France. Young men rushed to sign up. In 1798, when the festering troubles in Ireland erupted into open revolt, the Leicestershire Militia wrote to the king offering its services. On September 5th, 550 men marched out of Leicester towards Holyhead, taking with them 36 wagons, two pieces of artillery, and their 19 year old colonel, the Duke of Rutland.

In these years it was dangerous to voice any opinion which might be construed to be revolutionary. Two brothers who hung a red nightcap out of the window to tell the milkman to call, found themselves accused of republicanism.

A more serious victim was Richard Phillips, a mathematics teacher who had set up as a printer and bookseller on the corner of Gallowtree Gate and Humberstone Gate. He was a member of the Adelphi Club, which originally discussed scientific ideas, but soon turned to radical politics, much to the alarm of the corporation. Phillips began to sell revolutionary pamphlets in his shop. The local justices paid a shoemaker to buy a copy of Tom Paine's Rights of Man, and then prosecuted Phillips for selling seditious literature, although several other shops stocked the book.

Phillips spent 18 months in Leicester Gaol, and on his release a fire spread from a neighbouring house, destroying all his books and printing equipment. He moved to London, founded a literary magazine, and became a respected publisher. When he became Sheriff of London, he reformed some of the worst abuses of the criminal system, and undertook some early statistical research which showed that 49 out of 50 offenders were illiterate. He received a knighthood from George III.

The saddest outcome of the persecution of Leicester radicals concerned a friend of Richard Phillips, Mr Harley Vaughan, who was a master at the Free Grammar School. Vaughan was seen reading a handbill about a Reform meeting in Manchester, which had been handed to him by a coachman. He passed it on to someone else, and as a result spent three months in the Borough Gaol for sedition. When he was released, having lost his job, he walked out to the fields, tied his legs together, and drowned himself in a pit.

There was no Luddite machine breaking in

Leicester, but in 1817 six young Nottingham laceworkers who had raided Heathcote and Boden's factory in Loughborough were publicly hanged in Infirmary Square. Many in the crowd of 15,000, which included patients at the Infirmary, sympathised and joined the men in singing a hymn before they died. Apprentice surgeons at the Infirmary were given the bodies for dissection.

Enthusiasm for machine breaking died with the Luddites, and the knitting industry entered its worst period. Wages dropped to 6 shillings (30p) a week, from which frame rent still had to be paid. Many families had to ask for Parish relief, leading to soaring rate demands which impoverished others. The only solution was to increase wages, but hosiers maintained this would force them out of business.

The Combination laws forbad working men to form any sort of club or hold any kind of meeting with the purpose of improving wages or working conditions. All the same, in 1817 East Midlands hosiery workers managed to organise a strike. Leicester magistrates, themselves concerned at the sufferings of the poor, treated the matter tolerantly, but the strike petered out after a few months, defeated by lack of funds and the failure of a stockingers' co-operative scheme.

The Rev Robert Hall then helped the framework knitters to set up a Friendly Society. Such societies were legal, but were supposed to deal only with sickness and unemployment benefit. In Robert Hall's scheme, men paid 6d ($2^1/_2$p) a week when they were in work, and drew 8 shillings (40p) when out of work — even if they were not working because they were on strike. To all intents and purposes it was a union, but it was hoped to evade the law.

The next strike was so orderly and peaceable that it was held up as a model of its kind. In Leicester not a window was broken, not a violent action witnessed (though some rougher places like Mountsorrel and Shepshed were unable to restrain their men from attacking strike-breakers). The strike was deemed a success, and wages rose for a time, but the hosiers complained they were being undercut in an overcrowded market, and wages slid down again. Indeed, sixteen Leicester hosiers became bankrupt in 1819.

Those who made traditional fully-fashioned stocking complained that they were being undercut by makers of cheap cut-ups. Instead of the stocking being shaped on the machine and then joined in a safe, firm seam, a straight piece of knitted fabric was cut to shape and seamed. The stockings looked the same when new, but when they were washed they lost their shape and tended to unravel at the seam, for they were not overlocked.

In 1819 the framework knitters petitioned Parliament to prohibit cut-ups. One of their leaders, William Jackson, told a Commons Committee that, by working 15 hours a day, he could earn 8 shillings (40p) a week. Three of his young children made 9 shillings (45p) between them, while his wife and a very young child did some seaming and made an additional 17d ($7^1/_2$p). After struggling to keep out of debt on less than £1 a week, he was now unable to pay his rates.

The 1819 Petition, like an earlier one in 1812, passed the Commons, but foundered in the House of Lords, defeated by the laissez-faire belief that it was wrong to interfere with the natural course of industry. The bells of St Mary de Castro tolled in mourning.

Again, the stockingers had gained nothing but sympathy, and increasingly came to believe that Parliament itself needed reforming. The immediate, and apparently insoluble, problem was that wages would not rise until there were fewer people in the knitwear industry, for there was always someone, in Leicester or elsewhere, so desperate he would take on work at any price.

Despite its concern for the stockingers, the corporation's main pre-occupation was with keeping its own party in power, locally and in Parliament. Only freemen could vote, so in the 1820s the corporation set about enrolling enough suitable new freemen to ensure continued Tory rule. A committee compiled a list of people who were considered sound. They were informed of their election and told they need only pay £3 stamp duty, other costs being covered by the corporation. They did not have to live in the borough, and nearly a third of the 800 new freemen created lived outside the county — many of them in Nottingham, where a Whig corporation was doing the same thing in reverse and enrolling men from Leicester.

The 1826 Parliamentary election was seen as a disaster. The main national issues were the Corn Laws and Catholic emancipation. In Leicester, where there was strong anti-Catholic feeling, £60,000 was spent on entertainment by candidates and their supporters, with much attendant drunkenness and rioting. There was no secret ballot, so there was plenty of scope for intimidating the electors. The voteless mob made their presence known by pulling up cobble stones in the Market Place (assisted by the special constables sent to control them) and pelting the magistrates, who retreated into the Exchange. The militia were called out, and the cavalry arrived. The officer in command called on everyone to disperse or be liable for transportation. A voice in the crowd cried out 'What do I care about being transported? I've had no work for five months, and now I'm half starved.' 128 people were arrested, but only nine came to trial and they were merely bound over to keep the peace.

Both the Tory candidates were safely elected, though only half the new honorary freemen actually voted, and the corporation had to mortgage some

*The Corn Exchange, in the Market Place — scene of riots and unrest in the 18th and early 19th centuries.*

property to pay its £10,000 debts. What is more, the newly elected MP Robert Cave changed his mind and voted for emancipation once he reached Parliament. The Catholic Emancipation Bill was passed in 1829, allowing Catholics to hold public office if they took an oath denying the Pope's right to interfere in British affairs.

◆◆◆◆◆◆◆◆

As well as political violence, there was plenty of straightforward crime in the town. In 1832 a famous murder took place. James Cook was a 21 year-old bookbinder with a workshop in Wellington Street. After he went home for the night, his neighbours found his chimney was on fire. They gained entrance and found that a large chunk of meat in the grate had set the chimney alight. When Cook arrived he said it was dog meat which had gone off. The neighbours were dubious, but no magistrate could be found, so Cook was allowed to go home.

The meat turned out to be part of the remains of John Paas, a tool cutter and engraver from London. This was deduced from some bloodstained trousers and a pencil case engraved with the letter P, but by then Cook had walked to Loughborough and caught the stage coach to Liverpool. Two Leicester officers were sent in pursuit, and caught up with Cook just as he was being rowed out to a ship bound for America. He jumped overboard, but was captured while swimming ashore.

He stood trial in Leicester on August 8th and pleaded guilty. He said he had hit Paas on the head to avoid paying 12 shillings (60p) he owed him, and when he tried to escape, he kept hitting him till he was dead. Having spent all day cleaning up the shop and burning the body in pieces, he had thrown the last piece on the fire and gone home. Had he stayed long enough to prevent his chimney from catching fire, he would probably never have been caught.

30,000 people witnessed James Cook's execution at 9.30am on August 10. Afterwards his body was displayed in an iron gibbet which was hung 33 feet high at the junction of Saffron Lane and Aylestone Road. In three days 20,000 people had been to see it, and the authorities, concerned by crowd behaviour, took the body down and buried it beneath the gibbet. This was the last time a gibbet was used in this country, and the irons which contained the body of James Cook can be seen in the cells at the Guildhall.

◆◆◆◆◆◆◆◆◆

Until 1835 the governing body of the town was composed of 24 aldermen and 48 common councilmen. The aldermen elected the councilmen, and the councilmen elected the aldermen, for life, out of their own number. The system was completely closed, so, as every member was a Tory, no member of another party stood any chance of being elected. Council accounts were not made public.

Parliamentary reform in 1832 was followed three years later by the reform of municipal corporations and properly elected councils. Only a minority of people had the vote, but it was a more democratic system than before.

The first local elections were held on Saturday December 26 1835. Most of the old councillors could not even gain nomination, for the Tories' only hope was to distance themselves from yesterday's men. The result of the election was a completely new council, containing only four Conservatives, none of whom had been members of the old corporation — whose final act was to award themselves hefty sums out of public funds.

The town was now in the hands of worthy, middle-class Nonconformist Liberals. The next seven mayors were members of the Great Meeting, which became known as the Mayors' Nest. Feasting was a thing of the past, and much harmless merriment was thrown out with the bathwater of corruption. Much of the town plate was sold off, including the gold mace which had been bought in 1649 to replace the one lost at the Siege of Leicester. It was bought by a publican, who displayed it at his inn, and was bought back by the council in 1866 for £85.

◆◆◆◆◆◆◆◆◆

The 1835 Municipal Corporations Act required the setting up of borough Police Forces. The old hotchpotch of Ward Constables and Parish Watchmen could not cope in a town where burglaries and street brawls were common, so the council appointed Frederick Goodyer, of Peel's New Police Force in London, to take charge of a force of fifty officers. Mr Goodyer installed his family in the house in the Guildhall courtyard, with the Police Station and cells close at hand. The cells sometimes contained as many as seventeen prisoners at a time.

The new policemen became a familiar sight in

their blue tail coats and top hats, armed with truncheons and rattles. They were not universally popular, and some saw them as a waste of money and a threat to liberty. In the first year, 116 people were charged with assaulting the police, and there were 15 attempts to rescue people who had been taken into custody. Drunkenness was a major problem — among the police, as well as the public.

When the Rural Police Act allowed the establishment of county forces, Frederick Goodyer was given the more lucrative position of first Chief Constable of Leicestershire. He moved his headquarters to the three-storey Georgian building opposite the Saracen's Head in Market Place South, near the City Rooms.

Leicester by this time boasted a very secure gaol in Welford Road, designed in the style of a medieval castle, complete with arrow slits and portcullis. It is far more impressive than the real castle.

Growing congestion in the town brought increased risk of fire. In 1834 a group of businessmen set up the Leicestershire Fire Insurance Company, with two engines and trained firemen. Eight years later it moved to a purpose built, classical style Fire Station (later the Goldsmith Record Library) in Welford Place, designed by William Flint.

Private Fire Brigades would only turn out for subscribers, who identified themselves by hanging special plaques on the wall. The demand for their services lessened as the corporation's own fire-fighting arrangements improved.

◆◆◆◆◆◆◆◆◆

Meanwhile, the plight of the stockingers was not getting any better. In 1838, a new reporter joined the local Whig-Liberal newspaper, the Leicestershire Mercury. His name was Thomas Cooper, and he was horrified by the conditions he found. When he was sent to cover a Chartist meeting, the knitters told him they earned four and sixpence (22p). He

thought they meant per day, but they meant per week. He remembered how he had once, as an unmarried shoemaker, earned 10 shillings (50p) a week and considered himself poor. He also heard how the New Poor Law refused outdoor relief and sent those in need to suffer the deliberately harsh conditions of the new Workhouse in Swain Street. He became a convert to Chartism, a reform movement of working men.

The second Chartist petition to Parliament in 1842 contained a record 3,317,752 signatures. Among other things, the Chartists demanded the vote for all men, secret ballots, and the abolition of property qualifications for MPs, who should be paid, so that working men could be candidates. Most middle-class people, still terrified of Revolution, considered these demands highly dangerous: the frightening thing about workers was the vast number of them.

Thomas Cooper became one of Chartism's most famous leaders. He was dismissed by the Mercury, so he took over the local Chartist paper, and from his

*Leicester Gaol, built in 1828, is now one of the country's top security prisons.*

High Street office he sold leftish literature, bread and coffee. As conditions got worse in the Hungry Forties he led hunger marches through the streets. He tried to lead Leicester into the 'physical force' wing of the movement, but a strong local faction clung to the ideal of moral force only. He travelled around the country, supporting strikers and preaching Chartism, until he was predictably sent to prison.

◆◆◆◆◆◆◆◆

Occasionally a framework knitter prospered and set up as a hosier, renting frames and supplying yarn to other knitters. One such was the father of John and William Biggs. When their father died in 1827, the sons continued to build up the business. They were radical Liberals and members of the Great Meeting. After the success of the Parliamentary reform movement, they turned their attention to other issues: the end of church tithes, the repeal the Acts which prevented nonconformists from holding public office, and the repeal of the Corn Laws, which benefited farmers at the expense of consumers. It was a heady time to be a young radical.

William was the first to gain political limelight, while his elder brother John concentrated on the business. This was so successful that at one time the Biggs brothers owned nearly a thousand stocking frames, and employed a twelfth of the county's hosiery workers. When William overworked himself into a breakdown, his brother John came to the fore. Over the years each of them was three times mayor of Leicester and three times returned to Parliament.

In 1839 the Chartists called for massed meetings to be held in all big towns on Whit Monday. In some places terrified authorities armed the police and formed citizens' bands. When the Chartist leaders came to Leicester, however, they were received courteously by the magistrates, and offered the use of some land at the corner of Belvoir Street and Albion Street by John Biggs — not far from where his statue now stands, paid for by the subscriptions of working men after he died in 1871. The Chartists declared they had never met a kinder or more liberal gentleman.

In the Hungry Forties, though, unemployment and malnutrition brought even more misery and discontent. Employers were sympathetic, but were often facing bankruptcy themselves. Even John Biggs was heckled when he tried to address a meeting. He had always had his enemies on the right; now he had critics on his left as well. Working men were impatient of well-fed middle-class leaders, however well-meaning, who told them that the law of supply and demand meant that wages would sometimes go down, and people would sometimes be out of work. The poor stockingers, whose children were crying of hunger, could not take a long view. If it came to Revolution, they had nothing to lose but their miserable lives.

# Chapter 10 : Banking and Transport

*N*ew inventions alone did not make Britain the first industrialised country in the world. There also had to be improvements in transport and financial organisation. Businesses needed capital, and raw materials, coal and finished goods needed to be moved over long distances.

Banking evolved to suit local needs. At first traders and manufacturers helped each other as best they could. One early Leicester financier was John Watts (whose grandson founded the Infirmary). He came from Northamptonshire in the early 18th century, built Danett's Hall, and made himself very useful to rising hosiers. In the process he amassed a large fortune, most of which was lost by his son in the South Sea Bubble.

The early banks were usually set up by people who already had another trade, like John Mansfield, who had a draper's shop in Gallowtree Gate. He was an alderman and MP, and the exotic banquet he gave at the Guildhall when he became mayor was long remembered. So many people were invited that some of the local gentry had to eat upstairs in the library, from which hundreds of books had been moved. Years later, they were still lying about in confusion.

Banks tended to have a fairly short life, and nearly a third of English banks went out of business during the financial crises caused by the French wars. Leicester's Bellairs' Bank failed in July 1814. The partners were declared bankrupt, but their creditors were fortunate, being paid in full over two years. In the 1825 crisis, the senior partner of Miller's Bank was seen early one morning pushing a wheelbarrow full of coins from his home to his High Street premises, in case of a run on the bank. Miller's Bank weathered that storm and survived until its owners retired in 1835.

The longest lasting Leicester bank was that

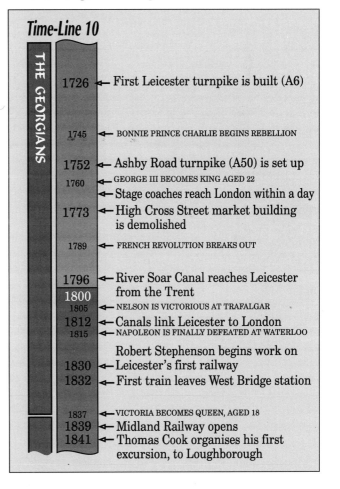

**Time-Line 10**

THE GEORGIANS

1726 ← First Leicester turnpike is built (A6)

1745 ← BONNIE PRINCE CHARLIE BEGINS REBELLION

1752 ← Ashby Road turnpike (A50) is set up

1760 ← GEORGE III BECOMES KING AGED 22

← Stage coaches reach London within a day

1773 ← High Cross Street market building is demolished

1789 ← FRENCH REVOLUTION BREAKS OUT

1796 ← River Soar Canal reaches Leicester from the Trent

1800

1805 ← NELSON IS VICTORIOUS AT TRAFALGAR

1812 ← Canals link Leicester to London

1815 ← NAPOLEON IS FINALLY DEFEATED AT WATERLOO

Robert Stephenson begins work on
1830 ← Leicester's first railway

1832 ← First train leaves West Bridge station

1837 ← VICTORIA BECOMES QUEEN, AGED 18

1839 ← Midland Railway opens

1841 ← Thomas Cook organises his first excursion, to Loughborough

established by solicitor Thomas Pares and his son, also Thomas. In 1776 the family bought four acres of the old Grey Friars land, including a building facing St Martin's, which they used for a bank. Pares' Bank thrived for over 100 years. In 1900 the building was replaced by the impressive structure now owned by NatWest. It is made of Portland stone, with two domed towers, ionic pillars, and friezes of classical figures. No new bank has been established in Leicester (other than branches from other areas) since 1829.

National Westminster Bank , St. Martin's, the site of Pares' Bank for over 100 years.

◆◆◆◆◆◆◆◆◆

The first improvements in communications came with the turnpike roads. The first in the county was the London Road (A6) from Market Harborough to Leicester and Loughborough. This was set up by Act of Parliament in 1726, with a loan of £150 from Alderman Newton. There were toll gates at the top of London Road and at the foot of Red Hill, Birstall.

The next turnpike, in 1752, was the road to Ashby (A50), but this was so badly laid out that most vehicles could get round the tollgates without paying. Within a short time, all the main roads out of Leicester were improved by Turnpike Trusts.

The first stage coach to London was organised by a Mr Needham. The coach, pulled by six black horses, left Leicester on Monday morning, reached London on Wednesday, and was back in Leicester on Saturday.

Better roads benefited markets and fairs, but the extra traffic brought its own problems to a town which still had narrow streets and medieval gates. The Highcross Street market house became something of an obstruction, and was taken down in 1773. The mayor in 1774 was Richard Drake, an auctioneer. He soon set about auctioning off the town gates, which were too low for loaded wagons.

Bulky and heavy loads, such as coal, were always a problem, even on the turnpikes. Leicestershire had its own coalfields, but unluckily they were on the far side of Charnwood Forest. For 700 years, packhorses brought coal across Leicester Forest, through Braunstone and along Coalpit Lane (now Braunstone Lane East).

In 1776 the River Soar was canalised between the Trent and Loughborough. This excited local industrialists looking for cheap transport, but gave

*Canalising the Soar, seen here at West Bridge, put Leicester on a heavy goods transport network, dealing mainly with coal, roadstone, and hosiery goods.*

nightmares to coal-owners, who could see Derbyshire coal coming to Leicester cheaper than they could supply it. They blocked plans to extend the canal to Leicester until a new cut was made, linking their coalfields to Loughborough. The resulting Charnwood Forest canal was a total and dramatic failure, with the collapse of the Blackwood Reservoir dam just the most spectacular of its disasters. Meanwhile the Soar Navigation was extended, and in 1796 Derbyshire coal reached Leicester. The price of coal fell from a shilling (5p) a cwt to 7d or 8d (about 3p). The coal owners' fears were realised, and some of them closed their pits.

Leicester was now a canal port, dealing mainly with coal, roadstone from Mountsorrel and Quorn, and hosiery goods. Improved transport and military orders brought about by the French Wars gave the knitting industry a brief period of prosperity, but this petered out after 1810.

England's canal network was completed in 1812, when the Grand Junction joined the midlands to London. Turnpike roads with their new macadamised hard surfaces now enabled flying coaches to travel at terrifying speeds, changing horses at roadside inns. The first steamboats were shunting around the coast.

The most glorious future, though, lay not with road or water transport, but with the railway. In 1815 George Stephenson patented his first steam locomotive, and ten years later he built a steam operated railway to take coal from Darlington to Stockton-on-Tees. In 1828 a coal-owner from Whitwick, William Stenson, went to see the new

wonder, and recognised its possibilities.

Back home, Stenson surveyed a route from the coalfields into Leicester, and took Quaker John Ellis as his partner. Ellis had met Stephenson, who was now working on the more ambitious Liverpool to Manchester Line. He travelled to Liverpool and found Stephenson in the Rainhill cutting, disgruntled by problems there, and not at all keen to go haring after another project. After a good dinner and a look at the map, however, he grew more enthusiastic, and set off for Leicestershire that very night, taking with him his son Robert.

The Stephensons went over the route with Ellis and Stenson, and afterwards called a meeting at the Bell Hotel in Humberstone Gate. The Leicester and Swannington Company was formed with a capital of £90,000, the first fifty £50 shares being bought by George Stephenson. Nearly £60,000 was subscribed, and local banker Thomas Paget agreed to lend £20,000. George Stephenson was asked to be chief engineer, but he was too busy and suggested instead his son Robert, aged 27.

Construction work began at the West Bridge

*West Bridge Station, the first railway in Leicester, has a restored platform, in Rally Gardens, Tudor Road.*

terminus in 1830, with the slate doorstep of the company offices as the base line. The major problem was the need for a tunnel near Glenfield. Early surveys suggested it would run through rock, but it turned out to be sand, needing a wooden framework to keep it in check while the brickwork was built. As a consequence, construction costs nearly doubled. When completed, the Glenfield railway tunnel was the longest in the world, at 1 mile 36 yards.

Amid great excitement, the first train left West Bridge Station at 10am on July 17 1832, drawn by the locomotive Comet, driven by George Stephenson. The $9^1/_2$ ton engine had been built at the Stephensons' Newcastle works, shipped to Hull and brought to Leicester by canal.

On its first journey the train carried about 400 people, including directors of the company, many of the most important townsfolk, and a brass band. Everyone had to sit on planks of wood in the open coal trucks. After a musical send-off. the train drew out of the station, but inside the tunnel it came to a

place where there was a mistake in the gradient of the line. The 13 foot high chimney struck the top of the arch and the train came to a sudden stop. The chimney fell down, showering soot on the grandees in their best clothes, and the band stopped playing. The engine managed to get underway again, and when the train emerged from the tunnel in Glenfield, there was a halt while everyone got out to wash in the stream and tidy themselves as best they could. Villagers who had gathered to see the train go by had more entertainment than they had expected.

Eventually the party arrived safely, if sootily, at the end of the line at Bagworth. Here they were entertained at several houses, and some of the men had a trip down a coalmine. On the return journey, some wagons were attached to the train, to bring coal to Leicester by rail for the first time. Before the next trip by the Comet, its chimney was reduced by six inches.

A few months later, the first accident occurred on the line. A train ran into a cart laden with butter and eggs which was using a level crossing at Thornton. The engine driver had a horn, but he could not attract the attention of the cart driver. As a result, the railway manager asked George Stephenson whether it would be possible to fit a whistle to the engine. Within ten days Stephenson had designed a steam whistle, and this became standard equipment on all locomotives.

The following year the line reached Long Lane (now Coalville). Collieries came back to life, including Coleorton, which had been closed for 30 years, and Snibston, owned by George Stephenson himself, which soon gained its own branch line. In Leicester a lifting bridge was built to take trucks across the canal to a coal yard in Soar Lane. The bridge was replaced by another of the same design in 1844, and this is now preserved in the Abbey Pumping Station.

The Railway Company's headquarters was at the West Bridge Station, on the site of the old Augustinian Priory. Originally there was no platform, and passengers had to clamber into the carriages as best they could. A new station was built in 1893. and part of its platform, edged with blue bricks, can be seen in the Rally Nature Gardens behind Tudor Road, together with a section of line, station name and signals. Passenger traffic ceased in 1928 and the Desford to West Bridge section closed completely in 1966. The rest of the line became part of the Burton-on-Trent to Knighton line.

Among the visitors at the railway opening were two coal-owners from the Erewash Valley in Derbyshire. What they saw convinced them that the canal trade was doomed, and led to the formation of the Midland Counties Railway Company. The project was taken over by wealthy Lancastrians, and to the fury of the coal-owners, the eventual route of the Midland line missed out the Erewash valley altogether.

When the Midland Railway arrived in 1839 it linked Leicester to Derby and Nottingham. Unlike the Swannington line, it was intended from the first to carry passengers. In 1840 it was continued to Rugby, and joined the line running to London's Euston Station. Long distance stage coaches and canal traffic declined.

The first excursion train to Leicester brought members of Nottingham Mechanics Institute to an exhibition at half fare. A week later the Leicester mechanics paid a return visit. The societies made their own arrangements, but their success encouraged the railway company to organise its own trips between Nottingham and Leicester. 2,400 Nottingham people booked tickets for a day out in Leicester and were packed into 65 carriages (divided into three classes), pulled by four engines. Crowds gathered at the Campbell Street station to greet the incoming train, which left Nottingham at 8.30am and was expected an hour later. When it had not arrived at 11.30, some railwaymen were sent in a spare engine to look for it. Half an hour later, another engine set off, this time carrying some of the directors. The missing train eventually arrived at 12.30, to be greeted by a crowd of 20,000 people and the Duke of Rutland's band. On its return journey, the train was divided into two portions, and arrived on schedule.

On June 9 1841 a Baptist preacher who lived at Market Harborough walked to Leicester to attend a temperance meeting. As he reached Kibworth, a great idea occurred to him. Could the railway be used in the fight against strong drink?

Thomas Cook was born in Melbourne, Derbyshire, in 1808. His father died when he was 4, and he started work at 10. By the time he was 20 he was a full-time Baptist missionary in Northamptonshire, but returned to his old trade of woodturning when he married. He threw himself tirelessly into the temperance cause. and was also (unusual for the time) against smoking.

As he continued his walk to Leicester, he began to plan a train excursion to a temperance fête in Loughborough the next month. The trip was a huge success. 570 passengers were conveyed to Loughborough and back for a shilling (5p) a head, with a band playing throughout the journey.

After that triumph, other groups began to ask Thomas Cook to arrange their excursions. On one occasion he took 3,000 children to Derby for the day to get them away from the 'sensual temptations' of Leicester races. He and his wife moved to No 1 King Street, in Leicester, where he could spend more time arranging tours.

The difference between Cook's tours and other excursions was that he was the first person to undertake all the arrangements and expense

himself, with meticulous attention to detail. He hired the train, sold the tickets, and accompanied the tour himself. Stories were told of other tours where hundreds of people spilled out into a strange town looking in vain for something to eat. Thomas Cook's passengers never went hungry, for he had taken a preliminary journey to sort out any problems which might arise. He produced a handbook for each traveller, explaining the route and pointing out notable landmarks. As the railway network grew, he set his sights further afield, taking groups to Scotland and Ireland. He invented the package tour, with hotel and travel costs all absorbed into one price. The name of Thomas Cook became famous throughout the land, and eventually the world.

After his son moved the travel agency headquarters to London, Thomas Cook retired to his grand house at Thorneycroft (244 London Road). He did not forget his birthplace, and built 14 cottages in Melbourne, three of them for retired Baptist ministers. When he died in 1892 the Times described him and his son as 'the Julius and Augustus Caesar of modern travel.... it is only the absence of a railway that prevents them from issuing tourist tickets to the moon.' He was buried in Welford Road cemetery, which had been opened in 1849 on part of the old South Field because the old churchyards could not cope with the growing population. Half the ground was consecrated for Church of England use and the rest left for dissenters like Thomas Cook.

Two years after its founder's death, the travel

*The frieze over the old Thomas Cook premises in Gallowtree Gate portrays the first 50 years of company tours.*

agency added an extravagant Victorian façade to its four-storey premises in Gallowtree Gate, near the Clock Tower. Although this is no longer used by the firm, the frontage still retains the wording '1841 T Cook & Son Ltd 1894', and a delightful frieze showing the development of the firm with parallel improvements in transport. 1841 is represented by an early train with open carriages; 1851 shows a less primitive train at the Great Exhibition at Crystal Palace. In 1884 Cooks are transporting their customers in a steam ship to the pyramids, while in 1891 a powerful train is shown approaching the Forth Bridge in Scotland.

Railways changed the face of Britain. When Victoria came to the throne, most people travelled only as far as they could walk, yet long before Victoria's reign was over, London could be reached in two hours and most of England and much of Wales and Scotland was accessible. The railway took pupils to school, businessmen to their offices, cattle to market, and families to the seaside. There were goods trains, passenger trains, mail trains, milk trains, royal trains, boat trains.... Railwaymen were the aristocrats of the working class, and most small boys dreamed of being an engine driver.

All this happened within the lifetime of some of the children who stood and watched the Comet draw out of West Bridge station for the first time.

# Chapter 11: The Victorian Town

Queen Victoria's coronation took place on June 28, 1838, and William Gardiner was in Westminster to witness the event. At 2pm, he records, a rocket was set off on the Abbey roof, announcing that the crown had been placed on the queen's head, and this was the signal for cannon to fire over London.

In October of that year, the Leicester and Leicestershire Political Union was formed to take up the cry for a People's Charter. Local Chartist leaders, such as John Swain, a framework knitter who had managed to buy a few frames of his own, and John Markham, a Methodist preacher, struggled to keep the cause active but non-violent.

While working people were rallying to Chartism, the middle classes were trying to abolish church rates and repeal the Corn Laws. In 1843, a new local conflict broke out over a proposed town improvement bill. The more cautious councillors, like wealthy worsted-spinner Joseph Whetstone, thought they should limit themselves to sanitary measures. The Biggs brothers and their like wanted to push ahead with a whole series of reforms.

In 1845 the Great Meeting opened the Leicester Domestic Mission, to undertake social work among the poor. Joseph Dare, who took charge, came to know more than anyone else about the health problems and living conditions of local people. He visited widely, issued annual reports, and pressurised the authorities for sanitation, building regulations and compulsory education. In 1846 Leicester appointed the first medical officers of any local authority in Britain in Dr John Barclay and surgeon Mr John Buck. A national cholera epidemic in 1848 hastened the passing of the Public Health Act, and a local Highways and Sewerage Committee and Board of Health were set up.

Once begun, improvement took on a momentum of its own and in a few decades the face of Leicester

**Time-Line 11**

THE VICTORIANS

| | |
|---|---|
| 1836 | Collegiate School is opened |
| 1837 | VICTORIA BECOMES QUEEN, AGED 18 |
| 1843 | Town Improvement measures begin |
| 1845 | First museum opens, on New Walk |
| 1851 | New shoe making methods introduced |
| 1853 | Stead & Simpson open Leicester's first shoe factory. Thornton reservoir comes on stream. Temperance Hall opens |
| 1862 | DJ Vaughan sets up working men's college |
| 1865 | Corah brothers build a knitwear factory |
| 1868 | Clock Tower built on old Coal Hill site |
| 1870 | School boards are set up by the Council. First public library opens |
| 1872 | Univ. Extension Society formed, which eventually became Leicester University |
| 1876 | New Town Hall is completed |
| 1877 | Wyggeston Grammar School opens |
| 1878 | Gimson's engineering business opens their 'Vulcan Works' |
| 1885 | Work begins on Beaumont Leys sewage works |
| 1899 | SECOND BOER WAR COMMENCES |

was changed by a torrent of new amenity, public health and education schemes. Health was the priority, for Leicester had a high mortality rate, particularly among children. The main recorded causes of death in 1841 were consumption and fevers, such as typhus, measles and scarlet fever.

Unlike some towns, most Leicester families had a house to themselves, and there were no cellar dwellings. But working folk lived mainly on a diet of bread and potatoes, and worked long hours in bad conditions. Worst of all, before 1850 there was no

sewage system. Builders and parishes made ad hoc arrangements, but if sewage was discharged anywhere it was into the river. In poor quarters there was just surface draining and open, overflowing cesspools. Wells were contaminated.

It is hard to believe that most people did not link the fever epidemics to the bad drains and the state of the water they were drinking. While medical authorities debated the subject, the number of children dying before they were one year old was increasing. In 1871 it reached 25%. Some blamed the drains and the terrible state of the river; others 'bad air', humid conditions and the poor physical state of the mothers, who therefore produced weakly children; yet others condemned mothers who went out to work, for child minders and busy mothers sometimes drugged children to keep them quiet, unaware of the terrible damage they were doing. When even the experts were baffled, no wonder parents grew fatalistic and attributed the regular loss of their children to the will of God.

At length a plan was formed to create a reservoir at Thornton and pipe water nine miles to Leicester. It was a bold step as no-one had piped water so far before (though Manchester got ahead with the actual construction). Some people worried that there would be no water left for houses at the far end of the pipes. However, the new reservoir was opened in 1853, and the system worked well. Builders were obliged to connect new houses to the public water supply, and further reservoirs were made at Cropston and Swithland.

Meanwhile, several miles of sewers were being laid beneath the streets. There were problems: when the river was in flood, water gushed up the

*The Abbey Pumping Station is now a museum of technology. The huge steam driven engines remain in working condition.*

overflow channels, spilling the contents of the sewers into cellars and streets.

The first sewage works was on the west bank of the river, near Abbey Lane. In 1885 a new scheme was begun on Beaumont Leys — the largest of its kind in the country. At the old sewage works, a great new pumping station was erected, designed by local architect Stockdale Harrison, who later designed the De Montfort Hall. Gimsons built the four giant beam engines, and these remain in place in what is now a museum of technology. A new treatment works opened in Wanlip in 1965.

Even with clean water and better drains, though, babies continued to die at an alarming rate, especially in the summer. And they were not just babies of the poor. It is a pity that no-one took much account of a report which noted that babies rarely died while they were being breast-fed. Weaning was the most dangerous time, especially if it happened in summer. Not until early in the 20th century was the danger of infected cows' milk understood. As the old pastures were built over, dairy herds were situated further away from town, and milk — untreated and uncooled — had to be brought in by horse and cart or train. A frail baby, usually given an unsterilised bottle, was an easy victim. After a milk depot was set up in 1906, infant mortality rates tumbled.

In one area of health care, Leicester became notorious for opposing the official line, and that was smallpox vaccination. From 1853 vaccination of all infants over four months old was compulsory. But, although everyone was scared of smallpox, terrible tales were told of the hazards of vaccination, which was by cowpox vaccine. Thousands of Leicester parents were prosecuted for refusing to have their children vaccinated. Most accepted the fine as just another tax; a few refused to pay and were sent to prison. An Anti-Vaccination League was formed, led by a Sanitary and Waterworks engineer, J T Biggs. It became a moral campaign and an election issue.

By law the town was supposed to have a vaccination officer, but as he was paid 'piece rate', and hardly any Leicester children were being vaccinated, the position lapsed. Instead, a system known as the Leicester Method was set up. The emphasis was hygiene in the home, and a female inspector (in effect, a health visitor) was appointed. When a case of smallpox was diagnosed, the patient was moved to a new Isolation Hospital on high ground off Groby Road. Contacts were kept in quarantine and clothes and bedding burnt. As there was never a serious epidemic, and the local death rate from smallpox was below the national average, everyone was very satisfied with the Leicester Method.

Education was almost as much in need of improvement as public health. The old Free Grammar School had struggled along for years in the old High Cross Street building, its reputation fluctuating with its master. The last headmaster went senile, and when he died in 1841 the school died with him, until it was resurrected by the Wyggeston Trustees in 1877. They built a new school on the site of the old Wygston hospital — now occupied by the Leicester Grammar School.

Alderman Newton's Greencoat School was doing rather better, but in 1834 plans were made to start a new Boys' School. £25 shares were offered at 5% interest, and each shareholder could nominate as a pupil a male relative over the age of seven. The new school, the Collegiate, was designed by John Grey Weightman and built in Prebend Street, off the London Road. Eighty pupils assembled for the opening ceremony in 1836, somewhat swamped by 900 guests.

Early enthusiasm among the Free Churches collapsed when it was learnt that only Anglican teachers would be employed, so the nonconformists established their own Proprietary School in the New Walk. The architect, Mr Hansom (famous for designing the Hansom cab), designed an impressive classical building with a great portico. Fees were £8 a year, plus an extra £1 if drawing and modern languages were studied.

Neither school lasted long. The Collegiate never recovered from a financial crisis in 1865. Part of the building was taken over by a recently widowed schoolmistress, Mrs Betsey Islip, who founded the Collegiate Girls' School, while the Wycliffe Congregational Church used the rest. In 1922 the school was taken over by the council and became the Collegiate Girls' Grammar School. After the re-organisation of Secondary Education in the 1970s, the school became subsumed in the Wyggeston-Collegiate Sixth Form College, and the building was put to various uses by the council.

At the behest of the Literary and Philosophical

*The school on Peacock Lane was built as the Wyggeston Boys'. After serving much of the 20th century as Alderman Newton Boys' it is now the Leicester Grammar School*

Society, the New Walk Proprietary School was opened in 1845 as one of the country's earliest museums. Most of the exhibits were of natural history, such as stuffed birds and animals, but later an Art Gallery was added.

There were several early 19th century Academies for Young Ladies, the best known being the one in Belgrave Gate run by Mary Linwood. Miss Linwood was nationally famous for her embroidered pictures, mostly copies of old masters worked on a frame in sections. She used worsted, some of which she dyed herself, and displayed her work in London and to the Royal Family. Some of her pieces, such as the large Woodman in a Storm, after Thomas Gainsborough, are owned by the Museums Service. When she died in 1845, aged 89, she was buried at St Margaret's, where she had already added her name to her parents' tombstone, with the words 'died in the 19th century'. Her friends arranged a memorial tablet inside the church.

One of Mary Linwood's proteges was John Flower, a gifted artist who, because of his father's early death, had to be apprenticed to a framework knitter. Miss Linwood arranged for him to study in London under Peter de Wint, and when he returned to Leicester in 1817 he set himself up as a landscape artist and drawing teacher. His delightful local scenes portray the town as it was before the coming of photography. He made a comfortable living from his studio and was able to have a house built in the fashionable area near New Walk, now 100 Regent Road. He was a member of the Great Meeting, but when he died in 1861, aged 68, he was buried where he had been baptised, at St Mary de Castro.

There were no public elementary schools in Leicester until the 1870 Education Act required the setting up of School Boards in areas where there was insufficient voluntary provision. Some children went to Sunday Schools, where reading and writing were taught along with Bible Study, but many were too tired after working 18 hours a day during the week. Some of them had to spend Sunday in bed, anyway, while their underclothes were being washed. A few churches, such as the Great Meeting and St Mary de Castro, had day schools, but if children went to school at all, it was usually only for a few years.

Not many working class parents were enthusiastic for education; some middle-class people hoped it might reduce the crime rate. By education they meant reading and writing, for which they were rebuked by the reformist Leicester Chronicle, who declared that reading and writing are no more education than a knife and fork are a good meal. There were other folk who believed workers should be trained only for their appropriate station in life. "We would not teach clergymen to weave stockings, nor a mechanic to read Greek," declared one speaker, evidently unaware that the stocking frame had been invented by a clergyman, or that a few keen working men were already learning Greek.

The Leicester Mechanics' Institute was formed in 1834 for the benefit of working men who wanted to continue their education in the evenings. The Upper Room of the New Hall in Wellington Street was rented, and a reading room provided with books, newspapers and magazines. After a few years, though, the project went into a long decline, partly because the two subjects bright lads were most keen to explore — politics and religion — were banned. There was a library of about 5,000 books, but the members had a disappointing inclination towards novels and history rather than science and ethics. After the closure of the Institute in 1870, the books remained and the New Hall became the town's first Public Library.

*Designed by Joseph Hansom, this classical building on the New Walk opened in 1836 as a non-conformist school. In 1849 the Town Council took it over, and turned it into one of the country's first museums. It retains its original stuffed animals and birds but also has among its exhibits fossils and dinasaur bones; an Ancient Egypt collection; porcelain; silver and glass; and an adjoining Art Gallery.*

The Rev D J Vaughan had greater success with his Working Men's Institute. One of the most influential figures in Victorian Leicester, Mr Vaughan became Vicar of St Martin's in 1860, in succession to his father and two of his brothers — a remarkable connection as it was not a family living; each presentation was made by the crown. He founded his Institute in 1862. For fourpence a week a man could use the library and attend as many classes as he wished; alternatively, he could attend just one class for a penny. Mr Vaughan remained President of what became the Working Men's College for over forty years. In time, women were allowed to join.

In 1872 Leicester was selected as a centre for a University Extension Society, which arranged lectures by visiting speakers. After the First World War this developed into University College and ultimately into Leicester University. Vaughan College continues in existence, housed above the Jewry Wall Museum, as Leicester University's Department of Adult Education.

Another enthusiastic champion of working lads was Mary Royce. Born in 1847, she had a good education and a privileged upbringing as the

*The 'Pork Pie Chapel' in Belvoir Street was built in 1845 as a United Baptist Chapel. Designed by Joseph Hansom (who also designed the Hansom Cab and New Walk Museum) it is now the Adult Education Centre.*

daughter of an alderman. In 1868 she started a Sunday School in an old stockinger's workshop in Sanveygate, but soon decided one hour a week was not enough. She began to meet her lads on Tuesday and Thursday evenings and help them with their general education. When the Sanveygate Mission was built, she moved there, and included classes in chemistry, anatomy, biology, geography, maths, French, Latin and Greek. She also took the boys rambling in Charnwood Forest, visited their homes

*The New Hall in Wellington Street, 1831. This neo-classical building housed the Mechanics' Institute and Leicester Literary and Philosophical Society. It became the first Free Library in the town, in 1871*

and arranged Saturday night socials to which they could bring their girlfriends and wives.

One day Miss Royce saw two cottages for sale in Churchgate. She bought them and built there the Royce Institute. When, in 1875, women were at last allowed to take medical degrees, she determined to be a doctor. She matriculated, then travelled to London each week to attend classes, always returning at the weekend for her boys' Bible Class. She did not find examinations easy and had several failures, but when she was 43 she was able to set up a brass plate announcing herself as Dr Royce. She practiced from her Institute, becoming very popular with local women. She charged a shilling (5p) for a consultation, but usually gave it back as the patient left. Her work lasted for little more than three years. She was only 47 when she died of an infection caught while attending a patient at the Workhouse Infirmary.

The Royce Institute did not die with its founder. She left a bequest which allowed it to be put on a more permanent footing, aided by a later one from her mother, who lived to be 90 and retained a keen interest in the work begun by her daughter. When Lower Churchgate was demolished in the 1970s, the Insitute moved to new premises in Crane Street, and continues to nourish the spiritual and social life of a cross-section of Leicester folk.

Pillars of Victorian society were concerned that working men should live a sober, decent and God-fearing life, and threw themselves enthusiastically into the Temperance Movement. It was fitting that the first building to receive pure water from Thornton reservoir was the Temperance Hall in Granby Street, which had opened in 1853 with Thomas Cook as its driving force. The building gave the town a much needed hall for concerts and public meetings. Charles Dickens and Mark Twain gave readings there, famous musicians performed, and there were long-remembered bazaars and amateur concerts. The hall is now gone, but next door Thomas Cook opened a Temperance Hotel, now a shop and offices at 121 Granby Street. The two lower storeys have been stripped of every interesting feature, but the top two floors retain their classical elegance.

In the 1870s the Temperance Movement was enthusiastically opening coffee houses where men could enjoy the same kind of social life they found in public houses, but return sober to their families. In the 18th century, coffee houses had been a resort of the elite, but as taxes on tea and coffee were reduced, ordinary people began to get a taste for them, though a cup of coffee could still cost as much as a pint of beer. Coffee houses sold tea, coffee and cocoa at a penny a pint, women were welcome, and customers could bring their own packed lunches. Snacks, newspapers and amusements were also provided.

The specially built premises were so attractive that the middle classes began to use them. As the better-off also deserved to be rescued from the lure of alcohol, the organisers began to cater for them, setting aside rooms for professional people, with higher prices to subsidise the rest of the operation.

Most of the coffee houses fell out of use during the First World War, when many of the men were away in less comfortable surroundings. Afterwards, the more genteel customers turned to the fashionable new teashops, such as Winns, which had branches in Gallowtree Gate, Granby Street and the Market Place. The Leicester Coffee & Cocoa House Company, which had once owned eight suites of premises, all open from 5am to 11pm, went into liquidation in 1921, unable to support any longer its most needy clients, who gathered to keep warm, buying only an occasional cup of tea, and asking for a plate and salt and pepper. Some of the handsome buildings remain, such as the Eastgates Coffee House, and the exotic Victoria, whose dome and turrets still rise majestically above the mundane shop windows of Granby Street.

◆◆◆◆◆◆◆◆◆

In the middle of the 19th century, most stockingers still worked in small workshops or at home. The wind of progress which had swept through other areas had almost left Leicester behind. Knitting frames often still produced just one stocking at a time, and differed only slightly from William Lee's original invention.

The few factories in town were concerned with spinning rather than knitting. One such was Donisthorpe and Co of Bath Lane, established in 1739 and the oldest factory still in existence in Leicester. Part of the building dates back to the second half of the 18th century, and can be best seen from the canal towpath, north of West Bridge. A good water supply is essential to spinners, and another firm, Whitmore's, built the factory by the canal on the other side of West Bridge, long used by

Pex, in 1848.

While knitters continued to work for next to nothing and pay their own overheads, there was little reason for a hosier to build and equip a factory. In 1844 there were an estimated 18,494 frames working in Leicester, and the following year William Biggs told the Parliamentary Commission on the condition of the Framework Knitters that some attempts had been made to introduce steam power, but to a very small extent, and he did not think it was likely to succeed. As late as 1863 he thought it unlikely that hosiery would ever become concentrated in factories, at least for quality goods.

Only two years later, in 1865, the Corah brothers built a model factory on four acres of land near St Margaret's Church. They installed steam-powered circular knitting machines costing the amazing sum of £100 each. The cost of making stockings was halved, and other manufacturers were forced to follow suit. In the 1870s frame rents were abolished and children sent to school. Hosiers lost income, and knitters lost their winders, seamers and general assistants.

Factories were clearly here to stay, but for a long while there was prejudice against factory work, even though wages were usually better than in the old workshops. Factories were dark, cold and noisy, and the worker had to fit into a system which took no account of his preference to rise early or late, or to have an easy start to the week and rush through the work from Thursday onwards. And all the time there was a foreman or supervisor watching over

*Donisthorpe's factory, the oldest in Leicester, was ideally placed for both a water supply and later canal access. Built in the second half of the 18th century, its site was previously occupied by the Black Friars (Dominicans).*

him. A stockinger may have been half starved, but he was his own man. A factory hand was just a hand. The rest of his body and mind were only needed to keep his hands going till the going-home bell sounded. While Leicester's late entry into large-scale industrialisation spared it some of the evils prevalent in northern towns, manufacturers complained that people were reluctant to tie themselves down to factory work.

Hours and conditions were improving. Women and young children could no longer be employed for more than ten and a half hours a day (that is, twelve hours less meal breaks), and some enlightened employers, such as Corahs, began to provide recreational facilities. Trades Unions became active and wage rates improved: by the late 1880s men in hosiery earned an average of 25 shillings and 6 pence (£1.27p), and women eleven shillings and sixpence (57p). The working mother was not a 20th century invention: most working class women either went to a factory or did outwork at home.

From the 1850s onwards, Leicester became more prosperous. This was mainly due not to the hosiery factories, but to the introduction – at last – of new industries. Glove making helped for a time, but the real break-through was the coming of boot and shoe manufacture.

There were always local shoemakers, but the first person in Leicester to organise the making of footwear in quantity, for sale in shops, was Thomas Crick, who had a workshop at 34 Highcross Street. In 1851 Crick introduced a method of riveting soles to uppers which was so much quicker than hand-sewing that within twenty years he had a thousand people working for him — many in small sheds and workshops, like the knitters.

Edmund Stead and Edward Simpson, leather manufacturers from Leeds, opened a factory in Leicester in 1853 and pioneered the use of an American invention, the Blake sole-sewing machine. They made Leicester the headquarters of Stead & Simpson, who combined manufacturing with setting up a chain of shoe shops. At first the shops were not expected to make a retail profit; their purpose was to ensure a market for the products of the factories.

The footwear industry took off in earnest in the 1870s, and soon there were seventy local factories. Thomas Roberts, for instance, came from Northampton in 1872 and set up a modest concern in the Newarke which became the Portland Shoe Works, with a reputation for high quality, comfortable ladies' shoes.

As machines became bigger and more complicated, most workers had to accept the discipline of factory life, but most Leicester firms remained fairly small family businesses.

The town's position on the railway network encouraged the growth of warehousing. George Oliver, who had been apprenticed to a shoemaker at Barrow-on-Soar, decided to concentrate on distribution. By 1889, Olivers and Stead & Simpson each had a hundred shops.

Once the snowball of ancillary industries began to roll, Leicester workers were in the happy position of having a choice of employment. Local hosier, Caleb Bedells, is credited with the invention of elastic web manufacture, incorporating rubber threads into a fabric during its making. Originally intended for braces, it was useful for the cuffs of knitted gloves, and really came into its own when elastic-sided boots became fashionable. The profitability of elastic web making was reflected in its sumptuous factories. Archibald Turner's Gothic fantasy in King Richard's Road is gone, but Faire Bros' warehouse in Rutland Street, which has been described as a Renaissance palace, remains.

The beginnings of Leicester's engineering

industry can be traced to the establishment of the Britannia Iron Works at the Belgrave Gate wharf by James and Benjamin Cort at the end of the 18th century. As well as turning out gas lamp standards, windows and gratings, they began to make the metal parts for hosiery frames. Corts' apprentices set up on their own: Samuel and William Pegg, and Josiah and Benjamin Gimson began by servicing local industry, while William Richards worked largely with the railways.

Gimsons opened their first engineering works at 36 Welford Road, and in 1878 they established the impressive Vulcan Works on three acres of land near Humberstone Road. Gimson apprentices, like Corts', set up as masters themselves. Josiah's son, Sydney Gimson, saw the need for highly trained technicians and was keen to set up a Technical College. This, together with a College of Art, was eventually established in the Newarke, becoming in time the Polytechnic, and now De Montfort University.

The ease of rail transport encouraged other firms to move to Leicester, including light and precision engineers such as T J Gent, makers of clocks and telegraphic instruments, and Taylor, Taylor & Hobson, well-known for their lenses. Charles Bennion, best known for giving Bradgate Park to the people, came from Cheshire and set up an engineering partnership which became the British United Shoe Machinery Company.

There are still many Victorian factory buildings around the town. Their box-like shape, with several floors, is determined by their original dependence on steam power. One steam engine provided power for the whole factory. It stood in an engine house which required a boiler and a great chimney. The power was transmitted to the machines by leather belts and pulleys. Belts varied in size from maybe two feet wide at the engine house down to $1^1/_2$ inches

for various machines.

Belts could be very dangerous if they broke, and it was the job of the mill-wright to check them constantly for wear. It was also dangerous for people to walk round while the machinery was in operation. An early health and safety requirement gained by the unions ensured that the main belt was disconnected during break periods.

With the change to electric motors in the 20th century, engines became progressively smaller: first one per floor, then one per bench, and eventually one per machinist.

◆◆◆◆◆◆◆◆

Leicester had no public transport until the 1840s, when horse buses began to pick up passengers at the Campbell Street Railway Station and take them to other parts of the town. The increased number of wheeled vehicles caused traffic jams in the narrow streets.

The old Assembly Rooms at Coal Hill fell into disuse with the opening of the Hotel Street building (now the City Rooms). The corporation, after much prompting, bought the site and earmarked it for improvement in 1859. They couldn't be persuaded to spend any money on pulling the building down until part of the cost was raised by a group of businessmen, but at last the site was levelled and paved. Then a new problem arose. A number of nasty accidents took place on what was now a large, open space across which horses, wheeled traffic and pedestrians made their way as best they could. What was needed was clearly some kind of traffic island.

Various suggestions were made: a statue; a street lamp; public toilets. Then the council received a petition bearing 195 signatures urging the building of a 'bold illuminated clock'. A 'sort of Gothic square tower' was suggested, surrounded by four statues representing Simon de Montfort, William Wygston, Sir Thomas White and Alderman Gabriel Newton.

It was pointed out that it would be a chance to show off the town's artistic taste to visitors to the Royal Agricultural Show, due to be held in Leicester in 1868.

Happy to find it was not expected to pay for it, the council approved the plan. The money was raised by public subscription, and a competition for the design was advertised. 105 entries were on open exhibition for a week, then a short list was chosen, and the winning design announced. It was by Joseph Goddard, a member of the clock tower committee, who belonged to a dynasty of Leicester architects. His grandfather, Joseph Goddard Snr, constructed the treadmill at the old Borough Gaol; his father, Henry, designed John Flower's house in Regent Road. Joseph himself later designed the Sun Alliance building in Town Hall Square, the Thomas Cook building in Gallowtree Gate, the Midland Bank in Granby Street and the Church of St John the Baptist. He also developed the Highfields Street area. His son, another Henry, designed St James the Greater, and his great-grandson trained at the Leicester School of Architecture before practicing in London.

The clock tower was not quite ready for the Royal Agricultural Show, so visitors had to study its taste-fulness through the scaffolding. Local clock-makers were upset to find that the clock itself was coming from Croydon. Only when the project was finished did people question the choice of statues. William Wygston and Alderman Newton were certainly well-known local people, but Simon de Montfort,

*The building of the Clock Tower in 1868 shows how the town centre had shifted east of the medieval walls. Joseph Goddard's design for a traffic island has given us Leicester's most memorable landmark.*

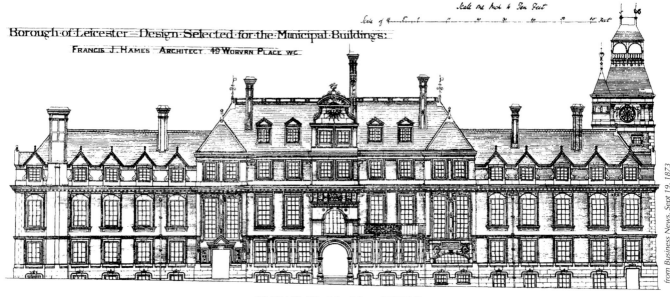

Borough of Leicester – Design Selected for the Municipal Buildings:
FRANCIS J. HAMES ARCHITECT 49 WOBVRN PLACE W.C.

*from Business News, Sept 19, 1873*

—— ELEVATION-IN-NEW-STREET. ——

despite being Earl of Leicester, left no recorded benefit to the town, and Sir Thomas White seems to have had no connection at all, apart from a general benevolence to young men from the midlands.

Once the new landmark was built, another debate began. What should it be called? Coal Hill was no longer favoured; Beneficent Place, Five Gates Cross and Guerdon Tower were among the suggestions. None of these names caught on, however, and by popular custom the area became known as the Clock Tower.

By now the old Town Hall (Guildhall) was hopelessly inadequate for a town which had grown by 40% in the 1860s alone, so other buildings were brought into council use. At the same time, there were endless complaints about the location of the cattle market in Horsefair Street. Herds of beasts had to be driven through crowded streets on market

*F J Hames' design for the Town Hall. The plans are dated 1873. The final design for the building, constructed three years later, involved various modifications, most notably to the tower on the right. The crest in the centre was also changed, to incorporate the Leicester cinquefoil motif.*

days. In the end, despite the opposition of butchers and dealers, who predicted disaster if the market moved away from the town centre, a new site was chosen between Aylestone and Welford Roads. This had direct access to the railway, as well as plenty of room for slaughter houses and other buildings. It continued in use until the 1980s.

The removal of the cattle market from Horsefair Street created an ideal space for a new Town Hall.

*Bishop Street Methodist Church, seen here beyond the fountain in Town Hall Square. The church was built in 1815 on cheap land alongside the cattle market. With the development of the Town Hall, 60 years later, it unexpectedly found itself in a prestige location.*

There was a design competition, which was won by an almost unknown Leicester-born architect, F J Hames. His dignified, red-brick building in a mixture of styles was considered too plain and restrained by those who would have preferred a full-blown Gothic extravaganza.

Like the new cattle market and some other large buildings, the Town Hall boasted a clock tower of its own. It was the heyday of the clock tower, for a world of trains and factories was a world which needed to know the time. Pocket watches were prized possessions, by no means universal, and needed to be checked regularly against a more reliable time-piece. Owners of public clocks could subscribe to a telegraph service from Greenwich which rang each day at 12 o'clock.

Despite its name, the Town Hall was really a block of council offices. No public hall was included, and the Temperance Hall continued to fulfil this function until the building of De Montfort Hall in 1913. The cost of the new Town Hall was £52,911, and it was formally opened on August 7 1876. The militia, military bands, firemen with their engines, police and councillors processed from the old Town Hall to the new, through streets lined with crowds of spectators, some of whom found vantage points on walls and roofs.

F J Hames also designed the fountain in Town Hall Square. This was paid for by Israel Hart, a Jewish clothier who was four times mayor of Leicester. (His brother was mayor of Canterbury.) With his partner, Joseph Levy, Israel Hart introduced mass-market tailoring to Leicester, and was active in the establishment of the Hebrew congregation. At first only occasional services were held, but as a result of migration from persecution in eastern Europe, a Jewish community grew up in Leicester, and a synagogue was built. When he died in 1911, Israel Hart (by then Sir Israel) left £190,000, which was a great fortune by Leicester standards.

The Guildhall was left empty for some time. Some argued it was old, gloomy and inconvenient, and should be pulled down, but the destruction of the old Wygston Hospital, next door. roused public opinion to the defence of its historic buildings.

Keeping the Guildhall was one thing; finding a use for it was more difficult. For a while it was a Cookery School, a purpose for which it seems particularly unsuited. At length, in 1922, a complete restoration was put in hand, and four years later it opened to the public. After 600 years of being at the centre of bustle, intrigue and (sometimes) corruption, it is now a tranquil retreat in the care of the Museums Service.

# Chapter 12 : Days of Queen and Empire

*L*eicester has not been the birthplace of many famous people, but just as in the 18th century it boasted the fattest man in England, in Victorian times it claimed the ugliest. Joseph Carey Merrick, born at 50 Lee Street in 1862, was known as the Elephant Man — a resemblance his mother attributed to having been knocked down by an elephant at the Humberstone Gate fair while she was pregnant. In fact, there was nothing unusual about his looks as a baby, but while still a small child his upper lip swelled, a bony lump grew from his forehead, his head became huge and his skin rough and loose. In time his feet and right arm became enlarged, and to make matters worse, he damaged his hip in a fall, which left him lame.

Joseph's mother died when he was 10 and his father married again. The boy was an embarrassment to his father and step-mother. His uncle Charles Merrick, who had a barber's shop at 144 Churchgate, looked after him for a while, but Joseph was unable to keep a job. He was in Leicester workhouse for three years, with 900 other paupers. He had an operation at the Infirmary to remove several ounces of flesh from his face, but no surgeon could do much for him, so the only alternative to the workhouse was to allow himself to be exhibited as a freak. He became the property of a syndicate which put on shows at fairs, and was advertised as 'The Elephant Man — Half a Man and Half an Elephant'.

By 1885 public opinion and regulations in Britain were turning against freak shows, though they were still popular on the continent, so Joseph was taken on tour, only to be abandoned in Brussels. After a nightmare journey to London, he collapsed at Liverpool Street Station, clutching a card bearing the name of Dr Frederick Treeves, who had previously taken an interest in him. Through public sympathy, Joseph was allowed his own rooms at the London Hospital, where he was taken up by the world of fashion, including royalty.

One of those who championed the disabled, and

## Time-Line 12

THE VICTORIANS

|  |  |
|------|-------|
| 1847 | ← Leicester's annual Whipping Toms and football game in Newarke stopped |
| 1861-5 | ← AMERICAN CIVIL WAR |
| 1869 | ← Leicester's first football clubs form |
| 1878 | ← Grace Road cricket ground opens |
| 1881 | ← Melbourne Hall Evangelical Church built |
| 1882 | ← Abbey Park opened by Prince of Wales |
| 1885 | ← Spinney Hill Park is laid out |
| 1891-2 | ← Rugby and Association Football pitches open on Welford Road & Filbert Street. London Road Railway Station opens |
| 1899 | ← Great Central Railway arrives |
| 1900 | ← Leicestershire Yeomanry join Boer War |
| 1901 | ← VICTORIA DIES, AFTER 64 YEARS AS QUEEN Western Park is opened |

helped to change the 'freak show' mentality was Dr Charles John Vaughan, a fashionable London preacher, and brother of Leicester's Rev David Vaughan, founder of Vaughan College.

Joseph Merrick read widely, and his real self began at last to emerge from behind the tragic mask that fate had bestowed on him. He was only 27 when he died, in 1890, from asphyxia caused by the weight of his massive head when he lay down in bed for once, like other people.

◆◆◆◆◆◆◆◆

Although Leicester was sprawling out into the countryside, until the 1880s it had only one small recreation ground, in Welford Road (now Nelson Mandela Park). Everyone agreed that more parks were needed, but the council held to the idea that land should be donated by generous benefactors rather than purchased out of the rates. Unfortunately, no such donors materialised. So, after flood prevention work on the river near the old Abbey grounds, it was decided to buy the land and lay it out for public recreation. There were many who opposed the scheme, either because it was a waste of money, or because it was considered an unhealthy site.

Undeterred, 66 acres were laid out with drives, lodges, greenhouses, a four-acre lake and an artificial hill. Rustic bridges

and bandstands were built, and 13,000 trees, plus shrubs, roses and flower beds, planted. There was a refreshment pavilion, tennis courts, and a bowling green, with adjoining pasture set aside for cricket. It was called Abbey Park.

Such a major undertaking deserved a special opening, and the Prince of Wales (later Edward VII) agreed to perform the ceremony, which took place on Whit Monday, May 29, 1882. When the royal

*Abbey Park from the air. The main gate from Abbey Park Road is in the top left corner of the picture, with the Abbey Mansion ruins just in front. To the right are the foundations of the Abbey, with the lake, bridge, and refreshment pavillion below.*

train arrived at Campbell Street station at 1pm, the Prince and Princess of Wales were greeted by a band and all the local dignitaries. A procession including their carriage made its way down Granby Street, past the cheering crowds. Near Dover Street, a man pushed forward and tried to shake the Princess's hand. The future Queen Alexandria tapped him on the wrist with her parasol and told him to go away, whereupon a mounted officer rode up and struck the intruder with the flat of his sword. The man was hauled off to the Police Station, where he was charged with drunkenness.

The royal route had been decorated with bunting and triumphal arches. There were stands to seat 25,000, but they were not full as the prices were too high. Many people preferred to follow the procession to the park, where another crowd was waiting. The Princess was handed a silver spade with which to plant a tree (or rather, to move the soil slightly

*London Road Station was built to serve the Midland Railway, in 1892. It is now Leicester's only Railway Station.*

before a real gardener with a real spade took over). The opening ceremony was performed on a platform in front of the pavilion (the predecessor of the present pavilion), and after refreshment and speeches, the royal party departed, leaving the townsfolk to enjoy fireworks in the evening.

Abbey Park was soon seen as an immense asset to the town, and in the following few years further parks were laid out at Spinney Hill (1885) and Western Park (1901). Victoria Park was formed out of the former race course.

◆◆◆◆◆◆◆◆◆

For 40 years or so, the only mainline railway through Leicester was the Midland. Its station in Campbell Street had at first only one platform, which was on a loop from the main running-lines, so southbound trains had to cross over the northbound lines. As traffic increased, this became unsatisfactory, so in 1868 the platform was turned into an island, with rails on either side. This solved one problem at the expense of another, for passengers now had to cross the rails to reach the platform. A fatal accident in 1872 led to suggestions such as a subway, as in some southern stations.

Other problems caused by lack of space and poor access made it clear that the only real solution was to build a new station. When the Great Northern Company planned its route, giving Leicester an easterly link, in 1874, it suggested a joint station to serve both lines, which would reduce costs and be convenient for passengers. The Midland toyed with the idea, but no action was taken. The suggestion arose again when the Great Central was planned. One railway station for all three lines would have been a great asset to businesses and travellers, but again the Midland Company could not bring itself to co-operate. In the end it replaced the Campbell Street station by the present one on London Road, while the Great Northern and Great Central were left to build their own stations away from the town centre, on less expensive land in Belgrave Road and Great Central Street.

The new London Road station was completed in 1892. Access was no longer at rail level, but from the bridge on London Road under which the trains entered and left the station. There were two large island platforms with waiting rooms, refreshments and books stalls (now all replaced), and a booking office at street level above. The council tried to persuade the Midland Company to provide sloping ramps to the platforms, but it refused to alter its plans, and the staircases became a problem to many.

London Road is the only remaining railway station in Leicester. (At some undefined moment in the 1970s, young people began to speak of train stations.) Visitors are sometimes puzzled by the arches on the façade labelled Arrival and Departure. Originally, a traveller would enter by the Arrival arch and use the booking office, then cross the bridge and descend the stairs to the platform. On return, he could take the stairs at the south end of the platform, which led directly to the higher of the two parking areas. Later these stairs came to be used by football fans, to segregate them from the rest of the travelling public.

The Great Central Railway, the last main line, arrived in 1899. The original plan was for the line to cut straight through the Jewry Wall and the Castle, but an outcry from the Leicestershire Archeological Society and others put an end to that idea. In the end, the railway was forced to cross the river, and the company had to provide public access to the Blackfriars Roman pavement beneath the station platform (now moved to the Jewry Wall museum). It also had to build 300 new houses to replace the homes it demolished, which was a useful piece of slum clearance.

The Great Central Line was built to perfection. Three-quarters of a mile of blue-brick viaduct, which cost a fortune and could have lasted for centuries, carried the rails across the town. The arches of the viaduct were used as workshops by small businesses. The line was part of Sir Edward Watkin's dream of linking the Industrial North to the continent via a channel tunnel. It was a brilliant scheme, but too late for the great railway days, and too early for the tunnel; it never paid a dividend on its ordinary shares. The line closed in 1969, though part of it to Loughborough has since been re-opened by a preservation society, again carrying passengers by steam locomotives. The demolishing of Leicester bridges (one, at least, of which was made of steel)

*The Great Central Railway was built to last for centuries, but closed after 70 years. To the south it is now the Great Central Way, a pedestrian and cycle route into the city. A few miles north of Leicester, steam trains once again ply the tracks to Loughborough.*

ended hopes of the line reaching the city again. Southwards from West Bridge, the track is now a cycle and walkway, known as the Great Central Way.

◆◆◆◆◆◆◆◆◆

A countrywide passenger transport network allowed regular sports fixtures to be arranged between far-flung teams, and nationwide leagues began to appear. There had been a Leicester cricket team since at least 1780. It played some exciting matches. In 1789 a match against Nottingham broke up in disorder after a dispute about following-on, and had to be finished some weeks later, when Leicester won by one run. From 1825, there was a ground in Wharf Street, where Leicester played local towns and villages, and occasionally more important matches. A representative Leicestershire team met Nottinghamshire for the first time in 1845 and Derbyshire in 1850, and these became regular fixtures. The last match at Wharf Street took place in 1860, when a Leicestershire 'Twenty-two' beat an All-England Eleven, before the land was sold for building.

For some years there was no regular ground, until, in 1878, the Leicestershire Cricket Association bought twelve acres off Grace Road. In their first season they invited the Australian touring team to play, being the first county side to issue such an invitation. When they played the Australians again in 1888, Leicestershire won. In 1895 they achieved the official status of first-class county, moving to Aylestone Road in 1901, but back to Grace Road in 1946.

Football was an ancient game, often played in the streets. It had few rules, any number of players, and a reputation for hooliganism. The annual game in the Newarke was stopped in 1847, along with the Whipping Toms.

The first proper football clubs in the town date from 1869, and in 1880 several clubs joined together to form the Leicestershire Football Club. It organised both Association and Rugby matches, which were played either on a ground in Belgrave Road or on Victoria Park. In 1884 the club divided into the Leicester Fosse, which played soccer, and the Rugby team, which retained the name Leicester Football Club. The latter soon adopted striped jerseys in green, red and white (distinguished by letters rather than numbers) and gained the nickname 'the Tigers'. The regular Christmas match against the Barbarians is a tradition going back to 1909.

Both football clubs moved to their present grounds (Filbert Street for soccer and Welford Road for rugby) in 1891-2. The Fosse joined the Football League in the 2nd Division in 1894. At first all players were amateurs; the first professional, Harry Webb from Stafford Rangers, joined in 1889 for two and six ($12\frac{1}{2}$p) a week. The club was re-named Leicester City when the borough became a city in 1919.

◆◆◆◆◆◆◆◆◆

Victorian Leicester was a strong church-going town, but mostly nonconformist. There were all the mainstream Free Churches, as well as various independent missions, some with imaginative names, such as the Fire Brigade of Jesus. As the town spread, churches opened in the new suburbs.

The Rev F B Meyer came to Victoria Road Baptist Church in 1874, but broke away from the Baptist establishment in favour of more unconventional evangelism. He started a mission in Infirmary Square, and by 1881 his supporters were able to build Melbourne Hall, on St Peter's Road. Mr Meyer worked mainly among the poor, and won hundreds of converts. He moved to London in 1888, but Melbourne Hall continued its evangelical tradition, drawing large congregations.

For those who wanted to question religious

belief, there was the Secular Society. After struggling to find a suitable meeting place (most halls belonged to churches) the Secular Hall was built in Humberstone Gate in 1881. Its meetings had much in common with churches, with a Sunday School, secular hymns to sing and a lecture instead of a sermon. The secularists held to a high ethical code, which was Christian in everything but belief. They were concerned about education and poverty and attracted social reformers. On the front of the Secular Hall there are busts of Voltair, Tom Paine, Socrates. Robert Owen and Jesus. These people were admired for having tried to build a better world, and for being ready to criticise the establishment of their time. The inclusion of Jesus as one philosopher among others upset many church people. The Secular Hall is the only such which still survives outside London.

Members of the Gimson family, who owned the Vulcan Engineering Works, were particularly involved in setting up the Secular Hall. They were also connected with the Great Meeting, and were more concerned to question religion than to destroy it. The Gimson home became a centre for the discussion of politics, religion and art.

Into this household, Ernest Gimson was born. In 1884, when he was 19, Ernest attended a lecture on Art and Socialism by the great William Morris. At the height of the Industrial Revolution, Morris was a leader of the Arts and Crafts Movement, which turned away from industrial processes. Morris believed furniture should be hand-made from solid English wood, rather than cheap wood with a fancy veneer. He believed in vegetable dyes for fabrics instead of the new chemicals. He was a poet, author, designer, and idealistic socialist.

After the meeting at the Secular Hall, William Morris went back to the Gimson home for the night, and sat up late talking to Ernest, his elder brother

Sydney, and his sister Sarah. It was a turning point in Ernest's life. He was articled to Isaac Barradale, the architect who designed the Joseph Johnson building (now Fenwicks) in Belvoir Street. Two years after his meeting with Morris, he left for London, with letters of introduction from William Morris. He joined several societies connected with the Arts & Crafts Movement. and met the Barnsley brothers (also called Ernest and Sidney), with whom he later worked.

During the 1890s Ernest Gimson designed several houses for his Leicester relations. Inglewood, in Stoneygate, is in red brick, with a Swithland slate roof. He originally intended it for his own occupation, and inside he decorated it with plaster friezes and William Morris wallpaper. The White House, also in Stoneygate, was built for Arthur Gimson. It is L-shaped, of limewashed brick and Swithland slate.

In the Ulverscroft area of Charnwood Forest, Gimson built Stoneywell as a summer retreat for his brother Sydney. It is on a sloping site with floors and windows at varying levels. Lea Cottage, close by, was built for Mentor Gimson, and was thatched and lime washed. Rockyfield, which is smaller, was built for his sister Margaret in 1908. His town houses are elegantly formal, but his cottages rise almost organically out of the surrounding rocky countryside.

While still working as an architect, Ernest Gimson was learning the craft of making plasterwork ceilings, and was also interested in rush-seated chairs. In 1900 he moved to the Cotswolds and set up a furniture workshop, producing designs which were made up by his craftsmen. According to his staff, his ideas always worked; they never had to say they couldn't do what he wanted with the materials he chose. Each man was allowed to make a piece of furniture from beginning to end, which gave pride in work, but was in complete opposition to one of the basic tenets of industrialisation: that products can be made at far greater speed, and therefore more cheaply, if each worker specialises in just one operation.

Gimson's original aim was to provide simple oak furniture to grace a workman's home. Unfortunately, there was an inbuilt contradiction in the Arts and Crafts Movement. Beautiful cottage furniture was made, but the ordinary cottager could not afford it, even when craft wages were low and the designer was prepared to live mainly on his private income. A small rush-seated chair could not be sold for less than £2, which was too much for most working people, who in any case generally preferred fashionable Victorian clutter to a few solid pieces of beautiful furniture. Much of Gimson's later furniture was less rustic, often in walnut or ebony, sometimes inlaid. A great deal of it was bought by his family, and there is a room at the Newarke Houses Museum devoted to furniture, plaster-work and metal-work from his workshop.

After Ernest Gimson's death in 1919, the

*The Singer Building, on High Street, was designed by Arthur Wakerley in 1904. It portrays an assortment of British Empire motifs.*

business was continued by his foreman Peter Waals. Prices had to be higher, because Waals had no private income, but he received several Leicestershire commissions, such as the ebony and mother-of-pearl lectern in Anstey Parish Church. Peter Waals became adviser on woodwork design at Loughborough College.

A different, but equally idealistic, architect of the period was Arthur Wakerley (1862-1931). He was a Methodist and a Liberal who became a local councillor at 19 and mayor at 35.

Byelaws passed in 1875 laid down minimum building standards, but these were often ignored and there were still occasional outbreaks of typhoid. In 1885 Wakerley bought five acres of brick pits in the Green Lane area, and began his plan to develop North Evington. This self-contained area eventually contained houses, factories, shops, bakeries, a bank, churches, and fire station. Everything except a public house, which the teetotal Wakerley did not consider an asset. In the town centre, he built the Singer building in High Street (1902) and the Turkey Café in Granby Street (1900). After the First World War, he produced a design for semi-detached houses which sold for £299 each.

◆◆◆◆◆◆◆◆◆

The end of the 19th century saw Europe engulfed by a wave of nationalism and imperialism. Most of the British Empire had been acquired absent-mindedly, to no particular plan. Industrialisation, however, brought competition for markets, and strong countries grabbed land wherever they could get it, particularly in Africa. In South Africa a quarrel simmered for years. Boer farmers, descendants of Dutch settlers, had trekked north from the Cape to set up Transvaal and the Orange Free State, out of the way of the British — but found that Britain, inspired by Cecil Rhodes, dreamed of owning most of the continent.

War broke out in October 1899. The Leicester Chronicle voiced the popular opinion that it would all be over in six weeks. A few thousand farmers were not expected to put up much resistance to the British army. Four or five hundred Leicestershire reservists were recalled to their regiments. There was no official send-off, but the mayor set up a relief fund for wives and families. At the end of the year, letters home spoke of a Christmas truce, church parades and festive dinners. Then the shooting started again.

The British public was shocked by early setbacks, and horrified to be seen as a bully by the rest of Europe, devoid of allies or sympathy. Support for the war hardened, and those who doubted its wisdom and morality were put to scorn.

In February 1900 a contingent of the Leicestershire Yeomanry set off from the Magazine at 4.15 am, amid a throng of flag-waving patriots occasionally raising 'three groans for Kruger'. The men arrived in Cape Town at the end of March.

For some time the Boers besieged the towns of Mafeking and Ladysmith. Ladysmith was relieved first, but Mafeking withstood 217 days of siege, its garrison commanded by Colonel Robert Baden-Powell, who became a national hero and later founded the Scout movement. Readers of Leicester newspapers were proud to learn that, though the men were reduced to eating horsemeat sausages, they could still organise billiards tournaments.

News of the Relief of Mafeking reached the town on the night of Friday, May 18 1900. Some sceptics held back until confirmation arrived on Monday, but most people ran into the streets, dancing and singing Rule Britannia and The Soldiers of the Queen. The following day the Gas Department band played patriotic tunes in Town Hall Square. Church bells peeled, banners flew, and people, horses, dogs and cats were bedecked with ribbons and flags.

Inglesant's furniture shop portrayed Baden-Powell surrounded by red, white and blue electric lights and the motto 'One of the Best'.

In Gallowtree Gate the crowd looked for a soldier to fete, and for a while made do with a postman, as the nearest thing in uniform. He was abandoned when some real soldiers came along.

On Monday children met in school to sing the National Anthem and to cheer the Queen and Baden-Powell. Then they were given the rest of the day off.

The war now turned Britain's way, with more excitement at the fall of Pretoria in June. This time the crowds were smaller and more given to drunkenness, with fireworks and flaming torches thrown around.

By this time, news of the first Leicestershire casualties was filtering back from the front. Five extra members of the Leicester Ambulance Brigade were given an heroic send-off by a large crowd at the station, where the mayoress presented each man with a lily-of-the-valley buttonhole.

The end of the war was thought to be close, but the Boers kept up guerilla activity, while the British burned their farms and put their families in concentration camps. The bitterness this caused did not cease with the end of the war in 1902, although General Smuts ensured that South Africa supported Britain in two World Wars.

◆◆◆◆◆◆◆◆◆

The closing years of the 19th century saw the rise of a new political force. The Independent Labour Party startled many people when it gained more than 4,000 votes in a Leicester by-election in 1894; it maintained that number at the general election the following year.

In the 1900 general election, the Liberals were divided between the 'imperialists' who supported the South African War, and the anti-war faction.

The Conservatives were all imperialists; they sang patriotic songs at their meetings and were in tune with the jingoistic mood of the country. Leicester returned a Tory MP for the first time in forty years. The ILP chose as their candidate a Scotsman named Ramsay MacDonald. He gained the seat at the next election, and later became the first Labour Prime Minister (though by then representing another constituency).

Victoria was Queen for 63 years, and few of her subjects could remember any other sovereign. On January 19, 1901, the Leicester Daily Mercury ran an editorial on The Health of the Queen, reporting that her Majesty was no longer taking her customary exercise, nor attending to business. Two days later, readers were told that the Prince and Princess of Wales and the Kaiser were hastening to her bedside.

Queen Victoria died on Tuesday January 22 1901 at Osborne on the Isle of Wight, at 6.30 pm. The news reached the Leicester Daily Mercury by telegram at 7.15, and it immediately published a special edition. Church bells tolled, flags were raised to half-mast, and blinds drawn. Within half an hour the news had reached most of the town.

As no-one in authority had ever dealt with the death of a monarch, procedure was uncertain. Musicians, at least, were prepared, with copies of Handel's Dead March in Saul to hand. At the Opera House in Silver Street, the first scene of Martha had just ended when the orchestra suddenly struck up with the Dead March. The audience realised what this meant, and rose to its feet. Then there was uncertainty. The orchestra remained in their places, and the second act eventually took place, but then the performance was abandoned.

Similar events were occurring at the Theatre Royal in Horsefair Street, with the Dead March played at the end of the first act of The Silver King, and the performance first resumed and then abandoned. The Tivoli Music Hall closed on hearing the news.

At the North Evington Market Hall, a large audience was assembled for a benefit concert for a soldier who had been blinded in South Africa. At 8 o'clock Arthur Wakerley mounted the platform, stilled the applause and announced that the Queen was dead. The audience rose as the pianist played the Dead March, then the people filed quietly out to the strains of Lead Kindly Light amid the Encircling Gloom.

By the following day, shopkeepers had changed their window displays to sombre hues, and soon reported that trade in coloured goods was practically at a standstill.

Edward VII was proclaimed King of Great Britain and Ireland, and Emperor of India, at St James' Palace on Thursday, January 24th 1901. Leicester had to wait for a copy of the proclamation to arrive by post the following day, then it was read out three times: at the Castle, on the balcony of the Town Hall, and in the Market Place (which was still an open space except on market days). A civic procession moved from one place to another, escorted by mounted police and a band playing fanfares and national airs.

The population was out in force, with an estimated 60,000-80,000 people in the Market Place. The queen was dead, but there was the excitement of a coronation to look forward to.

# Chapter 13 : The Twentieth Century

*L*eicester entered the 20th century greatly enlarged. Boundary changes in 1892 brought into the borough an extra 33,000 people from the parishes of Aylestone, Belgrave, Knighton, Evington, Humberstone and Braunstone. In every direction there were new streets of terraced housing, mostly let by private landlords, for council estates and mass owner-occupation were yet to come. Humberstone aspired to be a garden suburb.

Council housing began in 1900 with two blocks of tenement flats in Winifred Street, near the Infirmary (still occupied). There was opposition from councillors who considered the project 'socialistic', and hopes of rehousing some of the very poor foundered when the high building standards demanded by the Local Government Board led to rents of 3 to 5 shillings a week (15p – 25p).

As villages became suburbs, reliable transport was essential. There were already horse-drawn buses and trams. There had been an experiment with a steam tramway in the 1870s, but it took an hour and a half to cover $3^1/_2$ miles to Belgrave, so it was quicker to walk. Electric trams were a much better prospect, though the unsightliness of their overhead wires was a bone of contention. However, the corporation finally bought out the private Tramways Company and set about converting the tram services to electricity. The first vehicles, built in Preston, came into service in 1904. Their open-topped upper decks were garlanded with foliage on the opening day.

Trams were regarded with a mixture of affection and frustration. They obstructed other traffic as they stopped in the middle of the road to load and unload passengers, and worked best where new roads were built, such as Blackbird Road where they occupied the central reservation. The last Leicester tramcar went out of service in 1949, but one — Number 76 — remains in running order at the Crich Tramways Museum in Derbyshire.

Trolleybuses never found favour in Leicester. Motor buses were introduced in 1924, though

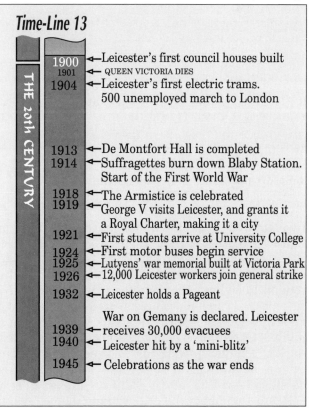

Time-Line 13

THE 20th CENTURY

1900 ← Leicester's first council houses built
1901 ← QUEEN VICTORIA DIES
1904 ← Leicester's first electric trams.
500 unemployed march to London

1913 ← De Montfort Hall is completed
1914 ← Suffragettes burn down Blaby Station.
Start of the First World War

1918 ← The Armistice is celebrated
1919 ← George V visits Leicester, and grants it a Royal Charter, making it a city
1921 ← First students arrive at University College
1924 ← First motor buses begin service
1925 ← Lutyens' war memorial built at Victoria Park
1926 ← 12,000 Leicester workers join general strike

1932 ← Leicester holds a Pageant

War on Gemany is declared. Leicester
1939 ← receives 30,000 evacuees
1940 ← Leicester hit by a 'mini-blitz'

1945 ← Celebrations as the war ends

*De Montfort Hall, completed in 1913, provided the town with a first class concert hall, with excellent accoustics. The controversy over its original cost was repeated at a major refurbishment 80 years later.*

horse-drawn drays and delivery vans remained a common sight until after the Second World War.

◆◆◆◆◆◆◆◆◆

A sharp recession in 1904-5 led to labour unrest. Five hundred unemployed men marched to London to draw attention to their plight. A large crowd saw them off from the Market Place, and they were cheered by wellwishers as they processed up the London Road accompanied by a new banner and a brass band. The march was organised by local labour leaders, including the Rev F L Donaldson, a notable Christian socialist who was Vicar of St Mark's. The group were not allowed, as hoped, to send a deputation to meet the king, but they attended services at St Paul's Cathedral and Westminster Abbey before walking home again,

arriving two weeks and a day after they set out. The trek had no immediate result, but it helped to strengthen the movement which led to the setting up of Labour Exchanges. Unrest in Leicester subsided with a further diversification of industry, especially in light engineering.

A well-known character of the time was PC Bobby Stevens, who was often on duty at the Clock Tower and said to be the biggest policeman in England. A picture postcard of him was produced. He would say to loiterers, "Do you play chess? Well, it's your move!" Then he would bump them along with his stomach. He died in 1908.

The Coronation of George V took place on June 22 1911, and a historical procession portrayed royal visits to Leicester from Ethelfleda onwards.

The town lacked a large public hall. The Temperance Hall was well used but it was privately owned. The council as usual argued fiercely about any project which cost money. At length a concert hall was decided on, and the firm of Stockdale Harrison was commissioned to build it. De Montfort Hall cost £21,000 and was completed in 1913. It can hold 3,000 people and the acoustics turned out to be excellent, making it one of the finest concert halls of its kind in the country. The organ was the gift of Alfred Corah.

In 1914, while people were still arguing about De Montfort Hall costing £3,000 more than expected, a new topic of conversation was the burning down of the platform at Blaby Station by suffragettes, who had been active in Leicester since the setting up of a local branch of the Women's Social and Political Union in 1903. Further afield there were troubles in Ireland and problems in Mexico and Albania. Then came the news of the assassination of Archduke Franz Ferdinand, heir to the Austro-Hungarian Empire, in a Balkan town called Sarajevo.

Rumours of war spread, with varying reactions.

Some folk were raring to go. The local Free Churches and the Independent Labour Party urged the government to stay out of war. Most people assumed it was just another crisis which would blow over, and went off to the seaside for August Week.

This time, however, Europe was skidding out of control. War was declared. People thronged to the Magazine to see the Territorials return from their holiday camps. Shops did well from those who could afford to stock-pile. A local school inspector, taking holiday snaps, was arrested as a spy.

Leicester was notorious because of the pacifism of its MP Ramsay MacDonald. Most people thought his views extreme, and cast him off at the next election, but the town was less enthusiastic for war than many others. After the initial rush, recruiting became a problem. Whereas in Nottingham 18.5% of men had volunteered by 1915, in Leicester the figure was only 2.6% (reflecting relative employment prospects in the two towns). As casualties rose, patriotic and emotional pressure drew more to enlist.

News from the front was censored, but filtered through slowly. Leicester became an important casualty reception centre, with over 60,000 men being brought here (514 died). The old lunatic asylum (now part of Leicester University), which had been empty for seven years, was hastily converted into a base hospital. Once the men started arriving, the town took them to its heart, knitting comforts and providing treats and hospitality for convalescents, many of whom came from distant parts of the empire like Australia, New Zealand and South Africa.

But for the heartbreaking casualty lists, many people found the war years personally fulfilling. Industry was humming: 70% of Corah's output went to the troops. Young women became nurses, transport workers or took over office or factory jobs which had been the preserve of men. Most of them had to relinquish their positions once the men came home, but never again could it be held that women were biologically incapable of coping with interesting jobs. In some spheres, such as office and secretarial work, women had arrived for good.

During much of the war there was no food rationing, just shortages and appeals for economy. Policemen sometimes had to keep order in the queues. When rationing did arrive, in 1916, it was at first organised locally, by a Food Control Committee. Leicester was the first place to ration meat, butter and margarine. National rationing arrived in 1918. That year the meat ration dropped from 10 oz to 4 oz per week, and hotels and restaurants had to have two meatless days a week. Through it all, though, the Prisoner of War Committee managed to keep all prisoners from Leicester supplied with weekly parcels of food, tobacco and clothing.

No bombs fell on Leicester, though ten people were killed in Loughborough during a Zeppelin raid. When news of the Armistice eventually arrived, after a day or two of rumours, children were sent home from school, factories closed, and crowds gathered in Town Hall Square and at the Clock Tower.

Fate, though, had another blow in store. A devastating influenza epidemic swept the country, killing 1,600 people in Leicester. Schools closed; undertakers could not keep up with their work, and the council lent staff to make hundreds of coffins at the Tramways Department.

A happier occasion occurred in 1919 with the first official visit from a reigning monarch for nearly 300 years. At De Montfort Hall, George V bestowed a knighthood on Alderman Jonathan North, who had been mayor throughout most of the war. Afterwards Leicester was granted a Royal Charter and was at last able to call itself a city.

*Built for the Wyggeston Girls School in 1878, this building was later used by the City Boys School and Charles Keen College. It is now Clarence House, the Age Concern building, its new rôle doubtless enjoyed by some of its former pupils.*

In the same year, the new Director of Education, F P Armitage, introduced a new examination for 11 year olds, and set about re-organising the provision of Secondary (that is, Grammar) Schools. The Wyggeston Boys moved to buildings which had been used for the military hospital near Victoria Park; Alderman Newton's moved to the St Martin's site vacated by Wyggeston (now Leicester Grammar School), making their premises across the road available for a new Alderman Newtown Girls' School. The Newarke School, previously mixed, changed to girls only, and the boys moved to a new City Boys' School, which met in the Great Meeting school until the Wyggeston Girls moved to Regent Road in 1928, when it took over their building in Humberstone Gate (now Clarence House, the Age Concern building). The number of Secondary places rose to 3,000 (150 free places a year) in 1923, and by 1939 nearly 40% of the children had free places. All schools for the over-11s were single sex.

Before the end of the war, the idea of a University — first mooted in the 1880s — was suggested as a memorial to the fallen. A fund was opened and in 1919 local manufacturer Thomas Fielding Johnson bought the old asylum for a University College. The first students — eight women and a man — arrived in 1921.

The sacrifices of the war were also commemorated by Lutyens' 1925 Cenotaph War Memorial, near De Montfort Hall. It is considered one of that distinguished architect's finest works.

The country was again in the grip of depression and unrest. In 1926, miners gained support from transport workers and a General Strike was called to start at midnight on May 3rd. Leicester council

*The Fielding Johnson Building at Leicester University. Built as a lunatic asylum in the mid 1800s, it became Leicester University College in 1921, and then a University in its own right.*

*The Cenotaph, designed by Edward Lutyens.*

formed a committee to run essential services and food distribution. It asked for volunteers, but stressed it was taking a neutral stance and not attempting to break the strike. On May 4th, the Leicester Mercury produced a small emergency edition headed 'Britain in Grip of Greatest Strike on Record'. Many factories kept working, but everyone was asked to reduce gas and electricity consumption by half, and only 350 street lights, instead of 8,000, were lit. The number of people on strike in the city on May 5th was 12,000. About twenty unions called out their members, and all Co-op employees came out.

It is an ill wind which blows nobody any good, and it happened that the first day of the strike coincided with the visit to Grace Road of the Australian cricket team. Despite lack of transport, ten thousand cricket fans turned up at the ground.

On May 12th the strike was called off by the TUC

Council. Traffic came to a standstill as motorists left their vehicles to buy newspapers. In public houses drinks were abandoned and overturned in the rush for the door when the call of the newsvendor was heard.

The railwaymen stayed out another couple of days and the miners refused to return, feeling let down by the TUC. At Coalville even the elements seemed to be against them, as they contended with heavy snow, a nine-hour thunderstorm and floods; in the end they had to give in.

After the strike, victimisation was the issue. Mr V M Taylor, of Taylor, Taylor & Hobson, declared his firm would not re-engage any striking worker. In some other places strikers were given only low-paid, menial jobs; others could find nothing at all.

There were 12,000 people on the books of the local Labour Exchange, with another 9,000 on short time. By national standards, Leicester was considered prosperous, but all things are relative.

The depression got worse before it got better, and in 1932 Leicester decided to cheer itself up with a pageant. This was a most ambitious affair, held on Abbey Park on every day from June 16 to 25 except Sunday, when a massed religious service was held

*Danes sail up the Soar to re-invade the town, as part of the 1932 Pageant.*

*from the Pageant of Leicester Official Souvenir, 1932*

instead. The logistics were formidable. Hundreds of people joined the cast and choir, and twenty committees took charge of every contingency from receiving visiting worthies to organising street decorations and illuminations. The pageant told the story of Leicester from the arrival of the Romans to the opening of Abbey Park. A great exuberance took over the city, and travellers on buses and trams grew used to sharing their seats with Saxons, Danes and Crusaders.

The first day of the pageant also saw the official opening of Charles Street, and a display of local industries at De Montfort Hall. Tuesday, June 21st, was designated Civic Day, to which all the Lord Mayors in the country were invited, and which was a special half-holiday.

◆◆◆◆◆◆◆◆

Just as the 1918 'land fit for heroes to live in' turned so soon into a nation of depression and unemployment, the yearning for peace led again to war in 1939. Leicester was considered low risk, so 30,000 evacuees were sent, mostly from London and Croydon, and later Ipswich. This was more than anywhere else in Britain. Most of them were children, in school parties, with labels attached to their clothes, clutching dolls, gas masks, suitcases and bundles. Most of the early arrivals went home again when the war started with a whimper rather than a bang.

The Second World War differed from any previous war. This was Total War, involving civilians almost as much as servicemen. There was a planned economy, with conscription, rationing, and direction of labour. Air raid shelters were dug, and those who were not being called up were badgered into joining the Home Guard, ARP (Air Raid Precautions), or firewatchers. There was black-out, gas masks, and ration books. Later, saucepans and iron railings were collected to be turned, supposedly, into spitfires.

The first bombs fell on Leicester on August 21 1940, during the Battle of Britain. A lone raider swept low through a break in the clouds and dropped eight bombs over the Aylestone Road Gasworks. They missed the gasworks, but killed six people in Cavendish Road, injuring many more. The air raid siren sounded when it was all over.

Because Leicester was considered a safe area, cinemas never closed, church services continued, and life carried on in a subdued fashion even after dark. The town was even allowed to have feeble street lights as, lying in a saucer of hills and often covered with light smog from house and factory chimneys, it was almost invisible from the air. On the other hand, it was not at first deemed necessary to spare any precious anti-aircraft guns for its defence, except for some wooden dummies intended to mislead observation planes.

During the devastating attack on nearby Coventry, stray raiders over Leicester killed two people in the West End and damaged both the City Football and the County Cricket Clubs. Five nights later, on November 19th 1940, Leicester suffered its own mini-blitz. This time the Tigers' stand was gutted, but the most affected areas were Highfields, where sixty people died, and Rutland Street, where fire destroyed the Freeman, Hardy & Willis factory and provided a target for further bombs. Aircraft on a course for heavily defended Coventry and Birmingham (which was hit by 350 bombers that night) turned to the blazing target, and eleven factories and warehouses and thousands of other properties were destroyed or damaged. A bomb crashed through the roof of the Town Hall, penetrated right down to the cellar, but failed to explode. The small fire which broke out was quickly extinguished by firewatchers with stirrup pumps. This was the only incident in Leicester which was allowed a mention on the radio. The only historic building to suffer was William Wygston's Chantry House, which was damaged by a High Explosive bomb.

The raid lasted 8 hours 17 minutes, during which time 108 people were killed and 203 injured. It was the first time Leicester had seen warfare first-hand since the Civil War in the 17th century. It had no raids of any sort after July 1941, when again Highfields bore the brunt, with one woman killed and seven people injured. Neither the flying nor rocket bombs reached Leicester.

Peace came to Europe on May 8 1945. Celebrations lasted for several days, with singing and dancing, street parties, bonfires and a few fireworks (either home-made or hoarded since 1939). A service of Thanksgiving in Town Hall Square was attended by 10,000 people, but marred by hail and a torrential thunderstorm. Three people who appeared before the magistrates for riding cycles without lights were let off.

◆◆◆◆◆◆◆◆

Life in immediate postwar Britain was marked not by depression, but by austerity (including the introduction of bread rationing, not known during the war), nationalisation and the birth in 1948 of the Welfare State.

There were festivities again in 1953 for the coronation of Elizabeth II. The old Humberstone Gate fair was revived, church bells rang and there was a civic service in Town Hall Square, though new television sets and chilly, showery weather kept many people indoors. Some cinemas installed special TV screens, and hundreds of pensioners were invited to view at the YMCA and the Co-op

Hall. An old gentleman at the YMCA said "I've been looking through binoculars and it's been perfect".

The 20th century saw a revolution in retailing. First there was the rise of the multiple store, with people increasingly buying their groceries at the local Co-op or one of the chain grocers such as Maypole, Home & Colonial, Lipton's and Worthington's — the latter being a local business founded in 1891, which during the Second World War had 49 shops in the city. After the war, the trend was first for Self-Service, then for modest supermarkets. Old familiar stores like Simpkin & James closed their doors for ever. By the 1980s American-style hypermarkets were opening all round the periphery of the town. The Co-op was the only local firm which could adapt to this trend, building hypermarkets in Thurmaston and Glenfield.

During the 1960s and 70s large areas of old Leicester were demolished to make way for new roads and high rise blocks. St Nicholas' Circle, the Underpass and the Holiday Inn took the place of Applegate Street and William Carey's cottage. Slums were swept away, but areas which had been full of life and character, like Wharf Street and Charnwood Street, were left with little sense of identity.

From the 1960s, Leicester became the

*The busy shopping street of Gallowtree Gate, with the line of the town walls down the left side of this picture, dates back to Danish times.*

*The Queen's Building, De Montfort University, is one of Leicester's newest prestige buildings. Built in 1994, it reflects the change in status from polytechnic to universty. Its position alongside the historic area of the Newarke finds strong echoes in its neo-gothic style.*

was a foreign language.

At length the pace of demolition slowed and conservation areas were created, including New Walk, the area behind the prison, and parts of Highfields. University College became Leicester University, and the Technical College became first the Polytechnic and then De Montfort University.

Leicester people still think the Clock Tower is the centre of the universe, and speak with a Danish-influenced dialect (even those whose parents came from Uganda or Barbados). Not that many Leicester people admit to having an accent at all — it's the rest of the country who talk differently.

Stand by the clock tower and watch the world go by. It is a richly cosmopolitan world. But then, it always was. Even the Corieltauvi came from somewhere else.

destination of many immigrants to this country. At first they were mainly Afro-Caribbeans, attracted by the post-war boom and full employment, and prepared to take lower paid jobs which employers found it hard to fill. Later incomers came from the Indian subcontinent and East Africa. Sari shops, Indian restaurants, mosques and temples became part of the Leicester scenery, while schools were challenged by an influx of children to whom English

# Bibliography

[TLAS – Transactions of the Leicestershire Archeological Society;
LUP – Leicester University Press; LRS – Leicester Research Services]
Allaway, A J, David James Vaughan, *TLAS*, 1957
Armitage, F P, *Leicester 1914-1918*, Edgar Backus 1933
Arnson, J M, *St Mary de Castro*, 1960
Ashley, Maurice, *England in the Seventeenth Century*, Penguin 1952
Banner, John W, *Discovering Leicester*, Leic City Council Info Services 1991
Beaumont, Richard, *The Beaumont Heritage 850-1972* (pub privately)
Bennet, J D, John Flower, 179301861, *TLAS* 1967
Bennet, M, Henry Hastings & the Flying Army of Ashby, *TLAS* 1981
Billson, C J, *Mediaeval Leicestesr*, Edgar Backus 1920
Billson, Charles James, *Leicester Memoirs*, Edgar Backus 1924
Bindoff, S T, *Tudor England*, Penguin 1950
Blank, E, *Ratae Coritanorum*, Ginn, 1971
Brandwood, Geoffrey K, *The Anglican Churches of Leicester*, Leic Museums 1984
Branigan K, *Roman Britain*, Readers' Digest, 1980
Briscoe, A Daly, *A Marian Lord Mayor, Sir Thomas White*, East Anglian Mag. Ltd, 1982
Brown, A E, (ed) *The Growth of Leicester*, LUP 1972
Carruthers, Annette, *Ernest Gimson & the Cotswold Craftsmen*, Leics Museums 1978
Chadwick, Owen, *The Reformation*, Penguin 1964
Clarke, David T-D, *Daniel Lambert*, Leics Museums 1950
Clough, Dornier, & Rutland, *Anglo-Saxon & Viking Leicestershire*, Leics Museums 1975
Crompton, James, Leicestershire Lollards, *TLAS* 1968
Cross, C, The Third Earl of Huntingdon & Elizabthan Leicester, *TLAS* 1960
Cross, C, *The Puritan Earl*, Macmillan, 1966
Cutting, Angela, *Leicestershire Ghost Stories*, Anderson Publications 1982
Elliott, M, Leicester Coffee House Movement, *TLAS* 1970
Elliott, Malcolm, *Victorian Leicester*, Phillimore, 1979
Elliott, M, Belief and Disbelief in Victorian Leicester, *TLAS* 1981
Elliott, Malcolm, *Leicester, A Pictorial History*, Phillimore 1983
Ellis, Colin, *History in Leicester*, City of Leic Publicity Dept 1948
Ellis, Isabel C, *Records of 19th Century Leicester*, privately pub 1935
Featherstone, Thomas, *Legends of Leicester*, J C Brown, 1838
Fielding Johnson, Mrs, *Glimpses of Ancient Leicester*, J & T Spencer 1891
Fosbrooke T H & Skillington S H, *The Old Town Hall, Leicester*, Edgar Backus 1925
Fox, Levi, *Leicester Abbey*, City of Leic Publicity Dept 1971
Frances, H J, Hugh de Grentesmesnil & his family, W Thornley, rep from *TLAS* 1924
Freebody N K, *History of Collegiate Girls' School, 1867-1967*, Armstrong-Thornley, 1967
Frizelle & Martin, *Leicester Royal Infirmary, 1771-1971*, 1971
Gardiner, William, *Music and Friends*, Longman 1838
Gill, Richard, *The Book of Leicester*, Barracuda Books, 1985
Gordon, W J, *Our Home Railways Vol 1*, Ian Allan 1910 (litho reprint)
Greaves, R W, *The Corporation of Leicester 1689-1836*, LUP 1970
Green, Susan E & Wilshere E, *Leicester Markets & Fairs*, LRS 1973
Green, Susan E, *Selected Legends of Leics*, LRS 1971
Gundry, D W, *Leicester Cathedral, A Short Guide for Visitors*, pub Provost & Chapter 1968
Hamilton, A and Broadfield, A, Chapel of Wyggeston's Hospital, *TLAS* 1973
Hamilton, A, Orthodoxy in Late 15th Century Glass in Leicester, *TLAS* 1980
Heydon, S, Provision of Medical Care for Poor in Leicester in 1830s, *TLAS* 1980
Hollings J F, *The History of Leicester during the Great Civil War*, Combe & Crossley, 1840
Howell, Michael & Ford, Peter, *The True Story of the Elephant Man*, Penguin 1980
Keene, R J B, *Architecture in Leicestershire 1834-1984*, Leics & Rutland Soc. of Arch. 1984
Kelly, William, *Drama & Amusements in Leicester*, J Russell Smith 1865
Kelly, William, *Royal Progresses and Visits to Leicester*, Samual Clarke 1884
Lee, Joyce, *Who's Buried Where in Leicestershire*, Leics Library & Info Service 1991
Liddle, P, Leics Archaeology, *The Present State of Knowledge Vol 1, to the end of the Roman Period*, and *Vol 2, Anglo-Saxon & Medieval Periods*, Leics Museums 1982
Lindley, Phillip G, *The Town Library of Leicester*, Ffynnon Press 1975
Lucas, J N, Town Walls: Evidence for a West Wall, *TLAS* 1979
Mellor J E & Pearce T, *The Austin Friars, Leicester* (CBA Research Report 35) Leics County Council & Council for British Archeology 1981

Millward, R, *Leicestershire 1100-1800*, Rep from Leic & its Region, LUP 1972
Mitchell, Tony, *A Newtown Trail*, Leicester Urban Studies Centre, 1982
Morgan, P, (ed) *Domesday Book, Leicestershire, 1086*, Phillimore 1979
Morris, Ernest, *The Prebendal Church of St Margaret, Leicester, A Short Historical Guide*
Myers, A R, *England in the Late Middle Ages*, Penguin 1952
Newman, A, Sir Israel Hart, *TLAS*, 1974
Old Union Canals Soc, *The Old Union Canals of Leics & Northants.*, 1967, revised 1982
Palmer, M, (ed) The Aristocratic Estate (Hastings), E. Midland Studies, 1982
Palmer, M & Neaverson, P, *Industrial Landscapes of the East Midlands*, Phillimore, 1992
Patterson, A Temple, *Radical Leicester*, LUP 1975
Pegden, N A, *Leicester Guildhall*, Leics Museums 1981
Pevsner, Nikolaus, *The Buildings of England: Leicestershire & Rutland*, Penguin 1960
Phythian-Adams, Charles ed, *The Norman Conquest of Leicestershire & Rutland: a Regional Introduction to Domesday Book*, Leics Museums 1986
Potts, G, New Walk in the 19th Century *TLAS* 1968
Pye, N, ed, *Leicester and its Region*, LUP 1972
Read, Robert, *Modern Leicester*, Winks & Son 1881
Ross, D L, Leicester and the Anti-Vaccination Movement, *TLAS* 1968
Royce Institute, *The Founder, Dr. Mary Royce*, privately published 1969
Semeonoff, Robert, *A Brief Guide to St Nicholas' Church*
Simmons, J, Thomas Cook of Leicester, *TLAS* 1974
Simmons, Jack, *Leicester: The Ancient Borough to 1860*, Alan Sutton 1974
Simmons, Jack, *Leicester Past and Present, Modern City*, Eyre Methuen 1974
Simmons, Jack, *Life in Victorian Leicester*, Leics Museums 1976
Skillington, Florence E, *The Plain Man's History of Leicester*, Edgar Backus 1950
Skillington, F, Trinity Hospital, *TLAS* 1974
Snow, E E, *Cricket Grounds of Leicestershire*, Assoc of Cricket Statisticians, 1988
Squires, A & Jeeves, M, *Leicestershire and Rutland Woodlands Past and Present*, Kairos Press 1994
Stanley, C R, Frederick Goodyer, Leicester's First Chief Constable, *TLAS* 1976
Storey, John, *Historical Sketch of the Borough of Leicester*, W R Lead 1895
Stretton, C E, *Notes on the Leicester & Swannington Railway*, Spencers 1891
Stretton, C E, *Early Tramroads & Railways in Leicestershire*, Tresise, 1900
Tanner, Michael, *Crime & Murder in Victorian Leicester*, Anderson 1981
Thompson A H, *The Abbey of St Mary of the Meadows, Leicester*, Edgar Backus 1949
Thompson, James, *The History of Leicester*, J S Crossley, 1849
Thompson, J, *Leicester Castle*, Crossley & Clarke, 1859 (facsimile, Sycamore Press)
Thompson, James, *The History of Leicester in the 18th Century*, Crossley & Clarke 1871
Thompson, A Hamilton, *The History of the Hospital and the New College of the Annunciation of St Mary in the Newarke, Leicester*, Edgar Backus 1937
Todd M, *The Coritani*, Duckworth 1973
Twining, Alison ed, *An Early Railway (The Leicester & Swannington)* Leics Museums 1982
*Victoria History of the County of Leicester*, Univ. London Inst. of Hist. Res. Vol II, 1954; Vol III, 1955; Vol IV, 1958.
Watts, Susannah, *A Walk Through Leicester 1804* (reprinted LUP 1967)
Williams, Daniel, ed, *The Adaptation of Change*, Leics Museums 1980
Williams, David, *Leicestesr & Leicester before 1870*, Leics Schoolmasters Assoc 1960
Williams, D T, *The Battle of Bosworth*, LUP 1973
Wilshere, J, Plague in Leicester, *TLAS* 1968
Wilshere J & Green S, *The Siege of Leicester 1645*, LRS 1970
Wilshere, Jonathan, *William Gardiner of Leicester (1770-1853)* LRS 1970
Wilshere, Jonathan, *The Town Gates & Bridges of Mediaeval Leicester*, Chamberlain 1978
Wilshere, Jonathan, *The Religious Gilds of Mediaeval Leicester*, Chamberlain Books 1979
Wykes, D L, Leicester Riots of 1773 & 1787, *TLAS* 1979
Ziegler, Philip, *The Black Death*, Collins 1969
**Newspaper files:**
Leicester Chronicle, 1898, 1899
Leicester Daily Mercury, 1900, 1901
Leicester Journal, 1900
Leicester Mercury, 1926, 1945, 1953, 1976
Leicester Mercury Supplements

# Index